CLEAR SPIRIT

The Life-Changing Power of
ENERGY CLEARING

JOANNE BROCAS

REDFeather™
MIND | BODY | SPIRIT

4880 Lower Valley Road, Atglen, PA 19310

To my husband, Jock, whose support in my life is truly beyond measure.

Other REDFeather Mind Body Spirit Titles on Related Subjects:
Creating Smudge Sticks, Peg Couch, ISBN 978-0-7643-5999-6
Feng Shui, Wu Xing, ISBN 978-0-7643-5886-9

Designed by Molly Shields

Young woman doing yoga exercise. © LerinaInk
Courtesy of www.Shutterstock.com
Type set in Arboria/Times New Roman

ISBN: 978-0-7643-6374-0
Printed in India

Published by REDFeather Mind, Body, Spirit
An imprint of Schiffer Publishing, Ltd.
4880 Lower Valley Road
Atglen, PA 19310
Phone: (610) 593-1777; Fax: (610) 593-2002
Email: Info@redfeathermbs.com
Web: www.redfeathermbs.com

For our complete selection of fine books on this and related subjects, please visit our website at www.redfeathermbs.com. You may also write for a free catalog.

REDFeather Mind, Body, Spirit's titles are available at special discounts for bulk purchases for sales promotions or premiums. Special editions, including personalized covers, corporate imprints, and excerpts, can be created in large quantities for special needs. For more information, contact the publisher.

We are always looking for people to write books on new and related subjects. If you have an idea for a book, please contact us at proposals@schifferbooks.com.

The information in this book is solely for informational purposes and is not intended to diagnose, treat, cure, or prevent disease or to provide medical advice. Please consult a licensed physician or other healthcare professional for your specific healthcare and medical needs or concerns. The content in this book is not intended to be a substitute for professional medical advice, diagnosis, or treatments. It is your responsibility to seek the advice of a licensed physician or other qualified healthcare provider with any question you may have regarding a medical condition and before undertaking any new healthcare regimen. Never disregard professional medical advice or delay in seeking it because of something you have learned in this book.

CONTENTS

INTRODUCTION

The Life-Changing Power of Energy Clearing

I was twenty-one when I passionately read through a variety of feng shui books, and right there and then my lifelong love of decluttering, space clearing, and energy healing began. During my early twenties, I got so determined to "clear the clutter" that I actually decluttered and gave away my feng shui books, which in hindsight was a little overzealous since I did miss them later on. I remember decluttering an old pair of my husband's football boots, only for him to notice them sitting neatly in the trash when he returned home from work. He immediately retrieved them as he shot me an irritated look. He'd been watching me "get rid of what we no longer needed" for many months. Roll forward twenty-eight years later, and I've not changed that much at all. If my husband leaves any kind of so-called clutter hanging around long enough, it's either likely to be given to Goodwill or placed in the trash.

Feng shui books were my early introduction to "energy flow" by learning how to rearrange the furniture in specific ways within the home in order to create a more harmonious flow of energy throughout it. The basic concept behind this is that when energy is able to flow more freely, without restriction and stagnation, then the overall vibrancy of the home is more healthful due to it being in greater energetic balance. A healthfully balanced home will provide the optimal energetic support for each person who lives there. Our own personal energies (which are an energetic mix of our mind, emotions, body, soul, and aura) are affected by the energies within our environment to varying degrees. This is based on the understanding that "everything is energy," both seen and unseen, both physical and immaterial. However, my even-earlier introduction to different kinds of energies began much younger for me, as a very small child. It was during kindergarten that I was taught a beautiful prayer that mentioned the angels watching over us throughout the night. I loved this prayer so much that I said it every night prior to sleep.

Prayer uttered with love and unerring focus on each word spoken, whether stated silently or aloud, naturally creates the necessary mystical experience to bless our mind, body, soul, and life experience with innate spiritual power. This kind of spiritual power is of the celestial kind—an important cosmic mix of Universal Light and Intelligence. What we therefore petition through our focused heartfelt prayers, we will always be given the exact vibrational answers required to meet our earthly needs. These vibrational answers can contain spiritual wisdom to help us gain a whole new perspective and understanding of some situation that will help to shift the whole dynamics around so that we can both resolve and rise above any challenges. Other vibrational answers may arrive in the form of healing as corrections and repairs are made to the energetic counterpart of our physical body to aid the body in healing itself. We may also receive intuitive guidance and spiritual leads to help us move forward in the best direction for us. Because of our prayer petitions, certain people may enter into our lives in order to help us with the next phase of our growth and development. In asking for help when we are emotionally low, we may then gain a feeling of renewed strength of spirit. Spiritual intervention is made available to us through the incredible power of prayer.

My sincere belief in my childhood prayer and my love of the angels naturally helped me expand my heart energy, which then awakened my consciousness further to experience a greater awareness of spiritual energies. I soon became aware of and much more sensitive to the energies emanating from people, animals, places, and spirits. I encountered the invisible yet tangible energies of spirits within my home environment. I was about five years old when I remember placing the palms of my hands up against a spirit's transparent hands and feeling the energetic pressure of them pushing right back. For some reason this incident didn't bother me in the slightest, yet later on, when I was about eight years old, I clearly heard a voice talk to me, which freaked me out because "there was no one there."

At thirteen, I read a book of real-life ghost stories. I was absolutely fascinated with these stories, and they certainly helped clarify some of the spiritual experiences I'd had in my early childhood. For several years prior to reading the book, I'd experienced a recurring dream about ghosts. In my dream I would find myself exploring a very large and beautiful home. Suddenly, I became keenly aware of the fact that I wasn't alone, and it was then that I noticed them, and they noticed me: the house was full of ghosts. They looked exactly like people except they had transparent bodies and their feet didn't touch the ground. As soon as these ghostly people noticed me, they began to move very rapidly toward me. I became surrounded by these ghosts, who were moaning for help with their ghostly arms outstretched. I had no idea whatsoever how to help them, and so I began to push them away, yet they continued to reach out for me. I panicked, turned around, and ran as fast as my dream legs could carry me toward the exit. However, I never did reach the exit, since I always woke up before I got there.

This dream lasted for several years, until one day it completely stopped. The dream I now believe was simply helping me spiritually awaken and prepare for a significant part of my life's work today. As a healer and energy expert I often assist human souls that are still attached to the earth realm to move onward to their rightful environment in the realms of Light.

At seventeen, I began my path of spiritual study and personal growth, and through this combination, my prayer life continued to spiritually mature and naturally evolve. My dedicated practice of daily prayers and meditations helped me heighten my intuitive awareness. At this time, I was also a trainee hairdresser and used to practice my intuitive skills on my clients. Washing their hair helped me connect to their personal energy fields, and so every time I asked them a question, I would also attempt to answer it within my mind before they did. Simple questions that I knew they wouldn't mind answering; still, it was a good way for me to refine my intuition and establish energetic connections. How many children do you have? Where are you going on your vacation? When are you going? What's your favorite food? Etc. And over time, I got really good at it.

Other hairstylists who knew that I was good at reading people's energy began to bring their clients to me before they got their hair washed, for me to do a quick impromptu palm reading for them. Seriously, I had no idea how to read palms; however, I did know how to read their personal energies by focusing my mind directly on them. Expecting their palm to be read, they thrust out their palm with eager anticipation and waited for "what I could see." Seeing absolutely nothing in their palm yet staring patiently at it, I was able to connect into their energy fields, also known as their aura, and gain some information and insight, of which they then verified with great delight. Police have often petitioned the help of psychics to do energy readings (known as the art of psychometry) on photographs, items of clothing, places, weapons, or objects that are involved in their ongoing investigations. While police dogs can zone in on the specific scent of a perpetrator, psychics can tune into the energetic signature of the perpetrator. This psychic energetic awareness is as real as the air that we breathe, and anyone can do it to varying degrees of skill. Some folks may take to it like a duck to water, while for others it may not come so easy, and more practice will be needed. Dedication to practice is what helps us strengthen and refine our intuitive skills.

In 2009, I became the nominated finalist for Best Female Medium in the British Spiritual Connections Awards. My intuitive connection with the spiritual realms, guides, and angels strengthened, and I wrote several bestselling books about angelic communication and healing. I continued to evolve and develop a deeper discernment and understanding of energy clearing, spiritual healing, and prayer. The reason for the name of this book, *Clear Spirit*, is because everything within our universe is made of energy that vibrates at specific frequencies. Energy-clearing treatments help clear energetic resistance that interferes with the integrity of a specific vibrational frequency. They help restore energetic balance and harmony back to an environment, a property, people, and animals.

Various methods of energy clearing have been used by different cultures around the world since ancient times as a way to clear, correct, and rebalance energy. Native Americans used herbs such as sage and cedar to smudge their environment. As the sage burns, the smoke is said to carry away any nonbeneficial energies and spirits. Crystals, sage, salt lamps, prayer blessings, ceremonies, geopathic shapes, and essential oils in diffusers are just some of the things that can help clear discordant and unbalanced energy within a space. While these offer wonderful ways to help us raise the vibrational frequency of a person and places to restore energetic harmony and equilibrium, this book offers another path to clear energy. Through the use of a simple tool called a pendulum (chapter 7), you will discover how to measure the overall energy of a home, person, or animal, along with using easy energetic techniques with a pendulum to clear energy and harmonize imbalanced energy. What if you don't have a pendulum? They are super easy to make, since all you need is a weighted object on a string, or you can simply skip the pendulum part altogether and just use the powerful energy-clearing prayer commands that you can adapt to suit you. Prayer power and pendulum energy-clearing techniques will help you take energetic charge of your home environment and personal energies so that you can take back your soul power and ignite a new level of spiritual freedom in your life. There is so much you can do energetically to help yourself and your loved ones with the wonderful energy-clearing treatments found in part 3 of the book.

How This Book Can Help You

This book will guide you in how to intuitively discern and understand the different kinds of energies that can adversely affect you, your home environment, and your family. You can then take and apply the clear steps and the creative solutions found within this book to help you restore greater energetic balance. The results of this can manifest as improved energy levels, improved health and well-being, increased joy, a new level of inner peace, harmonious relationships, increased abundance, and unlimited creative expression. When we are in energetic harmony with the energies of the universe and our home environment, then we will become more energized, joyful, and unlimited.

PART 1

Part 1 of the book includes chapters 1 to 5 and will introduce you to an array of energetic disturbances and the nonbeneficial energies that you can find within your home environment, and what I've termed "energetic clutter gutter." You will discover how these energies interact with your own personal energies and how the likes of "thought energy" is transmitted, which is easily explained by an MIT researcher. In chapter 2 you will discover that energetic residue is a significant cause of fatigue for many people due to them experiencing a buildup of emotional residue within the atmosphere of their home and work environments. You will gain some "ah ha" moments in how you can feel energetically drained. Chapter 3 will reveal information about energetic interference and the different kinds of factors and forces that impinge upon our energy fields and environment that can lower the overall vibrational frequency and resonance. Geopathic stress, technological stress, and other people's energies are just some of the energies that can adversely affect us. Chapter 4 deals with our personal energies and introduces aspects of our fascinating spiritual and energetic anatomy ready for you to work with when it comes time to do a personal energy-clearing treatment. Part 1 finishes with chapter 5, which reveals information about our house anatomy and the different ways in which our environment affects us and how we energetically affect it. You will read about the home's different kinds of energy fields, including the spirit guardian of the home. You will also find out how different colors can beneficially influence your home environment.

PART 2

Part 2 of the book includes chapters 6 and 7, and these offer you guidelines and knowledge about plugging into universal support for extra creative clearing power. Chapter 6 explains all about the outstanding power of prayer and the benevolent beings of Light that are happy to join their cocreative forces with you to greatly assist you in the energy-clearing work. Chapter 7 will reveal all about energy measurement and testing and will introduce you to the pendulum and its easy energy-clearing techniques. You will find a unique energy measurement chart to help you measure the energy of a person, place, or object before you begin an energy-clearing treatment, so that you can remeasure the energy once again afterward to notice any significant improvements.

PART 3

Part 3 of the book includes chapters 8 to 12, and they offer you a range of fantastic energy-clearing solutions to help change and rearrange energy. Through a variety of powerful energy-clearing prayers and specific energy-clearing steps and protocols, you will receive the necessary creative solutions that you can use to help clear, rebalance, and transform any imbalanced energies that are adversely affecting you. Part 3 will be a handy reference for you to refer back to the book anytime you should encounter a specific energetic problem. Solutions and methods are included in this part of the book to help you address the nonbeneficial energies of the home and work environments through in-person and distance energy-clearing work. Chapter 10 will be especially beneficial and exciting for those of you who have your own business or are ready to set up your own business. Chapter 11 is all about personal energy-clearing treatments, and they are specifically formulated to help bring you some remarkable results. Chapter 12 includes how to energetically clear your children, pets, and more.

It is my sincere prayer that the energy-clearing information, steps, and protocols you find within this book will help liberate you from your own individual stressors, prevent you from energetic fatigue, protect you and your loved ones from interference, and offer you a creative path to access unlimited spiritual freedom, joy, and abundance.

—JOANNE BROCAS

Personal Note: Throughout the book I use the terms "God," "Absolute Love," and "Divine Light" interchangeably. Please apply your own concept and version of Universal Intelligence in its place in order to suit your own personal and unique form of heritage, culture, and environment.

PART 1

ENERGETIC DISTURBANCES

CHAPTER 1

ENERGETIC CLUTTER GUTTER

If you want to find the secrets of the universe, think in terms of energy, frequency, and vibration.

—Nikola Tesla

Why Does My Home Feel So Unhomely?

Your home environment is much more influential to you than you may first realize. I don't just mean about the placement and arrangement of furniture as the Chinese art of feng shui teaches. Feng shui, also known as Chinese geomancy, is a system of laws considered to govern spatial arrangement and orientation in relation to the flow of energy (chi), and whose favorable or unfavorable effects are taken into account when siting and designing buildings.

I don't just mean about the life-changing magic of tidying up your personal space by decluttering and discarding what you no longer love, and keeping only what sparks joy, as the fabulous Marie Kondo suggests in her big hit Netflix series and her *New York Times* bestselling book. Your home environment is also a reservoir of invisible energies of different kinds that can impinge upon your own soul energies, physical body, and consciousness to affect you and others in a variety of ways.

Our thoughts, words, and emotions all create invisible energetic charges that leave their energetic imprints both in our personal atmosphere (the bio-auric field) and within the atmosphere of our home environment. While some of these energetic imprints will clear and transmute, the most-dominant, consistent ones can begin to accumulate over time to collect within our personal energies and to attach within the etheric space of our home environment. This accumulation specifically tends to happen within the areas of our home that we generally spend many hours of our life and time, such as our own side of the bed, a favorite chair, our home office, or some other sought-out favored spot. Invisible clouds of energy can linger in the air that contain pockets of personal information about what we've been creatively expressing. We naturally create and project beneficial energies, which are degrees of high vibrational energies, whenever we focus on and express our joyfulness, our positivity, our understanding, our compassion, and our kindness toward self and others. They are super supportive of our overall energetic vibration. This is because these high-vibe attributes are in harmony with our innate spiritual nature and heritage. We also create and project a variety of nonbeneficial energies, which are degrees of low vibrational energies whenever we focus on our dominant worries, fears, anxieties, and limiting thoughts. If we continue to hold on to any hate, anger, disappointments, and other kinds of low-vibe energies, then we become self-destructive, which adversely affects our overall energetic vibration. This is because these low-vibe energies are out of harmony with our innate spiritual nature. Nonbeneficial energies serve us as a platform for personal and spiritual growth and can be used as a springboard toward us transcending our limitations. Our irrational negative thoughts and feelings will often project in our imagination chaotic mental pictures, images, and visions of the dire life dramas and worst-case scenarios that could ever possibly happen to us or to our loved ones—just like a scary movie left on replay. It's therefore the accumulated nonbeneficial pockets and areas of discordant thought energy and emotional disharmony that are attributed to what I like to call "energetic clutter gutter."

What Are Thoughts Made Of?

This is what Charles Jennings, director of neurotechnology at the MIT McGovern Institute for Brain Research, says about what thoughts are made of:[1]

> They're really just electrochemical reactions—but the number and complexity of these reactions make them hard to fully understand. The human brain is composed of about 100 billion nerve cells (neurons) interconnected by trillions of connections, called synapses. When you read these words, for example, the photons associated with the patterns of the letters hit your retina, and their energy triggers an electrical signal in the light-detecting cells there. That electrical signal propagates like a wave along the long threads called axons that are part of the connections between neurons. When the signal reaches the end of an axon, it causes the release of chemical neurotransmitters into the synapse, a chemical junction between the axon tip and target neurons. A target neuron responds with its own electrical signal, which, in turn, spreads to other neurons. Within a few hundred milliseconds, the signal has spread to billions of neurons in several dozen interconnected areas of your brain, and you have perceived these words.

Thoughts and feelings don't just evaporate within the brain and body once they've been expressed. Their electrochemical reactions cause a shift in our body's physiology via our nervous system and our endocrine system. They therefore affect our brain hemispheres, cerebral spinal fluid, and hormonal balance to influence the well-being of our organs, systems, and body parts. We've all at some point felt the energetic effects of our thoughts and feelings directly influencing our physical body. Feeling embarrassed can cause our face to become flushed red with heat as blood rushes to the face and head. Our hearts will beat faster while watching a scary movie. Our throat aches when we express angry words during an argument. We experience goose bumps on our skin as a sensory reaction to some kind of conscious fear or due to some invisible type of energetic stimulus we happen to encounter within the environment. These physical responses are just a few examples of the energetic shifts that take place inside us due to our creative expressions and due to our sensitivity to the energies we directly encounter within our environment.

Any nonbeneficial energy contained within an environment that we happen to visit doesn't necessarily mean that it's going to be harmful to us, since we may be able to easily transmute it, and especially so if we aren't spending a whole load of time in that particular environment. We can also more easily transmute lower vibrational energies if our own personal vibration just happens to be strong, healthy, and in general good shape and resonance. In this sense, any adverse effects we may encounter are often only temporary, or they are very weak or even nonexistent. Other times, nonbeneficial energies can certainly adversely affect us in a variety of ways. This can be experienced as degrees of energetic drain, fatigue, impairment of mind, overall body weakness, heightened anxiety and mood swings, or aches and pains, among other issues. On a less physical and more subtle level of our being, we may also register nonbeneficial energy via our intuitive facilities in the form of a clear knowing and a gut instinct that something just doesn't feel right.

As well as causing an energetic effect in our body's nervous system and endocrine system, the electrical reactions of our thoughts and emotions also directly influence our body's spiritual and energetic anatomy. These are our meridian system (energy pathways), our chakra system (energy centers), and our bio-auric fields (energy bodies). Energetic imbalances within these systems can directly affect the quality and vitality of our physical health and well-being. Our chakras and our bio-auric fields transmit electrical waves of current directly into the atmosphere of our environment, as well as absorbing different kinds of energy from our environment. We will discover more about our spiritual and energetic anatomy in chapter 4.

Energy Patterns and Thought Forms (Energy Bubbles)

Over time, the same thoughts and feelings (thought forms) expressed within one particular area of our environment can begin to accumulate to such a degree that they create an energetic pattern with its own electromagnetic field of energy. Whenever we spend more time back there (maybe sitting in a favorite chair or spending time in an area of the kitchen, which is often known as the heart of the home), we also increase the possibility of us being directly influenced and triggered by this energy pattern and field. This is fine if the energy pattern and its electromagnetic field are predominantly positive, since we will feel uplifted, supported, and happy, maybe even triggering other happy memories for us. Supportive fields tend to build up in areas of the home where we creatively express higher vibrational energies. For example, participating in a meditation practice, doing some kind of daily spiritual routine, or doing something we regularly love to do in that space, such as reading, writing, art, playing the piano or some other musical instrument, dancing, singing, cooking, baking. These supportive energy patterns and fields can be thought of as power spots because they empower us.

If we happen to spend time in an area of the home where the energy pattern and its electromagnetic field are predominantly low vibe, then we will feel the opposite effects. Our mood may be unconsciously influenced to such a degree that within minutes of us sitting there, we begin to switch our minds into "worrisome mode." Hence the influential state of discordant energies resonating within the atmosphere moving and impinging upon us. We always have the free will to override this nonbeneficial influence; yet, if we are unaware that we are being energetically influenced, we will tend to think that it's our current mood and not "previous patterns of thoughts and emotions" that keep us locked into our personal energetic clutter gutter. Negative news stories, frustrating phone calls, checking on the state of the finances, other people's moods that we share the home with, our work deadlines, cleaning the home, and other task stress factors can all adversely affect different areas of the home environment. Do you have a particular room in the house where you go to have a secret scream or cry? (often expressed within the bathroom or while having a bath). While this can be quite cathartic in releasing your mental and emotional stress, the energetic effects of your emotional outpouring can accumulate within the space there. These disturbed and unsupportive energy patterns and fields are often known as weak spots because they can trigger us and weaken our energy.

To give you an idea of what thought forms are like when projected into a space, I like to use the following symbolic analogy. Think of an illustration of someone with a quotation bubble floating above their head, with certain words written inside the bubble to show them thinking and expressing specific thoughts and emotions. This is a great way to explain the phenomenon of thought forms that carry energetic information that can at times form into energy patterns and fields. Instead of the actual words and their emotional significance appearing inside the energy bubble, it is their equivalent energetic frequencies that manifest there that carry invisible energy clouds of information.

Energetic Atmospheric Mix

How many people share your home environment with you? All of your energies will be immersed together, combined into an energetic atmospheric mix that contain both the beneficial kinds and the nonbeneficial kinds of energy. Babies, small children, teenagers, adults, and pets—all transmit and absorb different kinds of energy directly into and from the home environment.

Babies and Small Children

Small children like to play very close to wherever their mother tends to be within the home environment, due to them being energetically immersed within the protective range of their mother's auric field. This is because they feel safe and comforted by their mother's signature vibration, especially after spending nine months inside their mom's womb growing and developing during pregnancy. If the mother moves too far away from the child and the child becomes temporarily out of range of their auric field, then the child can become anxious and start searching for their mom. It's often the case that the mom has children gathered around her feet while attempting to get many things done. Babies are comforted by their mom cradling them because they are immersed directly in the energy field of their mother's heart energy, and they feel safe and loved.

Energy lines (cords of attachment) are also naturally created and exchanged between parent and child due to their shared genetic inheritance. Adopted children will still have energy lines connected to their biological parents due to their genetics, yet they will also create and share new energy lines of attachment with those who become their adoptive parents. Energy is exchanged and flows between parent and child through these lines and is one reason why a mother can have a deep intuition about her child when something is wrong. It is also the case of when twins are separated by distance, and they can immediately sense that something has happened. Energy lines and exchanges are also created between us and our significant relationships that we share with others to different degrees of intensity. Our spouses, lovers, friendships, bosses, workmates, clients, students, etc. Yet, the one created between parent and child is ultimately the strongest.

Babies and small children light up the home environment with their innate joy and their inquisitive energy. Their energy is mostly clear, vibrant, and unconditionally loving as they begin a new life experience. However, they are also affected to some degree by the energies of their soul history, which is the aspect of their soul that is eternal and has gained multiple experiences, both positive and negative, in their journeys throughout the universe prior to this new incarnation.

Babies and small children are often spiritually sensitive to an array of invisible energies within their home environment. They can see the likes of ancestor spirits, angels, spirit guides, and other kinds of spirits appearing to them. Many young children also have the invisible imaginary friend. While some will certainly be the product of the child's imagination, others will be due to a real spiritual cause.

Teenagers

Due to their emerging independence, teenagers like to spend more time alone, and often in their bedroom. They are slowly preparing for adulthood, and their independence is leaning toward adventure and exploration of the world without wanting too much or any of their parents' influence. The energetic atmosphere of a typical teenager's bedroom tends to be filled with a mix of emotional angst, romantic and sexual thoughts, feelings of needing more privacy, and some anxiety, moodiness, and anger energies. Anger is often a way of them releasing pent-up emotional stress as they begin to deal with hormonal changes and experience new thoughts and feelings about their body and their sexual urges. Anxiety is often experienced due to the pressure of study, college, or plans for the future. Teenagers and young adults are often moody and emotionally reactive with their parents, while of course there are always exceptions to this. Teenagers who begin experimenting with alcohol and drug use can create chaotic energetic responses within their bio-auric field that can open them up to spiritual interference. Teenagers, due to their hormones raging and their experimentation with different aspects of physical life, can become more energetically attractive to spirit energies. This means that the home environment can also include ghostly inhabitants who coexist along with the family. Spirit energies and interference can be easily cleared, and you will find out how to do this in part 3 of the book.

ADULTS

Adults have the responsibility of taking care of the property, taking care of any children, paying the mortgage or rent, working and housekeeping, and all that goes on with creating and maintaining a safe and secure environment. Ongoing worry and anxiety about taking care of these needs and requirements will affect not only the energetic atmosphere of the home environment; it will also affect their personal energies. Worry and fear energy have their own energetic signatures that can interfere with the energetic resonance of our personal fields. The physical result of persisting worry and fear energy interfering with our personal energies can adversely affect the well-being of our lower back, hips, pelvis, legs, knees, and feet.

Married couples or life partners will also energetically share with each their own source of stress (as well as beneficial energies), due to their attached energy lines. This invisible energetic exchange can influence each other's moods and vital energy levels. Harmonious and supportive relationships that are quick to recover from an argument or disagreement do tend to naturally transmute much of the energetic stress exchanged between each other, since true unconditional love is a superb energy-clearing and healing frequency. Relationships that do not grow in consciousness and harmony together will eventually grow distant or apart. Arguments, moodiness, lack of emotional connection and support of each other, and staying in a relationship that's simply beyond repair will generate an inharmonious energetic atmosphere of negativity and angst for all who live in the home. Young children are especially sensitive and susceptive of their parent's relationship with each other, even when any discordance is initially hidden from them. Energy lines between people can be cleared to help restore greater harmony, inner peace, and joy. Part 3 of the book will guide you through this process.

PETS

Cats especially like to spend time in areas of the home that are not so energetically compatible for humans. They are able to transmute detrimental energies that would adversely affect the human system, and in doing so they help lessen its negative effects within the home environment. Pets are super sensitive to energy and to the invisible realms. Have you ever experienced a cat hissing at what seems like empty space? It can be unnerving! Has your dog barked at something invisible to you? Pets and small children will often absorb and reflect their owners' and their parents' stress energies due to their natural empathic sensitivity. Small children can experience this as sleep disturbances and nightmares, and they can become emotionally reactive by acting out and being generally high-wired due to their nervous system being overloaded. As children grow older, their energy systems are more able to cope with the sensitivity due to them becoming more grounded to their earth life and through establishing new energetic boundaries. Pets will often absorb and reflect some of their owner's health issues. If the pet is in general good health, then they will be able to transmute it. Sometimes, though, they can become sick. Doing an energy-clearing treatment for a pet can often bring remarkable results, just as it did for one dog who was diagnosed by the vet as having meningitis. Within twenty-four hours of having an energy-clearing treatment, the dog's health significantly improved. You will find out more about this in part 3 of the book.

With such an energetic mix of adults, children of different ages, and pets, along with the energies of any family members and friends who regularly visit the home, we can find ourselves influenced, emotionally triggered, and sensitive to the combined energies that have been accumulating and congested within our home environment.

SENSITIVITY TO ENERGY

People who are energetically sensitive and empathic will naturally react to different kinds of energies in different ways, more so than those of us who are less sensitive. Long-term immersion of nonbeneficial energies over many years can begin to weaken our energetic constitution, boundaries, and resistance. The practice of energy clearing can help bring our personal energies and our home environment into greater energetic balance. Personal energy clearings can train our nervous system to discern and deal with different kinds of energies in ways that will be more supportive to us. Also, the clearer and more high vibe our energy fields become, the more the lower detrimental energies that we encounter will no longer adversely affect us. Regular energy-clearing treatments can help us formulate an energetic constitution that is able to block out, transmute, or transform any adverse energies we encounter.

Rental Properties and House History?

What if you live in a rental property? As you can imagine, the amount of people who've occupied the home prior to you moving in would have left their own energetic stamp. When people move out of a rental property or any property, they leave behind traces of their own energy patterns. When you move in, not only are you taking on the energy of the property's signature vibration, you can also be influenced by any preexisting patterns still resonating there.

The next thing to consider is the furniture. If it's a furnished property, then it's not just about the quality of the furniture; it's also about the quality of the energy absorbed and embedded within the furniture. If someone was sick for a long period of time and spent lots of their time lying on the couch, then they will leave an energy pattern of sickness within the couch. If someone who rented the property before you did took drugs, was violent, or participated in black magic or any other kind of detrimental behaviors, then their energy patterns will influence the property's overall atmosphere, and especially so in the rooms where these things took place.

The amount of energetic clutter gutter resonating in a place is determined by whether you moved into a new build or an older property. However, even a new build will have a mix of energies present there to differing degrees, depending on how attached they are to the property. Whose? The builders, the owners, and even the realtors. You also have the energies of the land that the property is built on, and the energies of the surrounding area that can impinge upon the property, as you will come to discover through reading this book. Each property has its own energetic history, and if you are about to move into a rental property, a new home, or a new business premises, then you can clear the energetic atmosphere of the property and any nonbeneficial influences on it before you move in. This will certainly help with the settling-in process as you move into a new energetic environment and all that goes with it.

Low Energy and Negative Patterns

Some homes have problems selling due to the accumulated energetic disturbances existing there, or due to a disturbance directly affecting the property, originating from some nearby location. Such disturbances lower the overall vibration of the property and the surrounding area. A graveyard, hospital, or prison located very near to a property can create energetic problems due to them radiating their dominant low vibrational frequencies outward toward the property, land, and surrounding area. You only have to think about the energetic clutter gutter of such places to understand why their dominant energy frequencies are so low—a mix of human suffering, sadness, negative energy patterns, illness, and even spiritual interference. Realtors often find that one house in particular just won't budge and will stay on the market much longer than anticipated. Often this is the result of a property that has significant energy problems. Houses that have foreclosed will carry a negative energy pattern of foreclosure energy, plus the energy patterns of the family's emotional stress and financial stress leading up to the foreclosure.

There is a principle in feng shui known as the predecessor law. It recognizes that events that have previously happened in a property can happen again. Do you know of any homes or businesses that have experienced the same patterns there, yet with different occupants? One household I know of contained the energy pattern of divorce. The last three couples who lived at the property, one after another, had experienced relationship problems that led to three divorces. Other properties can resonate nonbeneficial energy patterns of sickness, financial hardship, and conflict that can continue to influence any new occupants who are vibrationally attracted and drawn to living or working from such a property.

Business premises that keep going bust will have the energy patterns of financial loss, struggle, and possible bankruptcy. These energy patterns will need to be cleared in order for a new business to have a fair chance of success. A restaurant kept changing hands in our local area even when the food was good and the staff were friendly. The restaurant was never as busy as other restaurants found within the same area. It's not always about the quality of the food and the friendly staff; people also need to feel energetically comfortable and happy within the building's atmosphere when enjoying a meal.

A place can lack the vibrational energy and power to draw people in and keep the business flowing. Have you ever walked into such a place and felt the atmosphere there as being heavy, dense, and flat? If so, you are intuitively registering the invisible energy patterns emanating there. Energy patterns become more firmly fixed and anchored whenever they are repeated. In the restaurant's case the prior business failures made the initial primary pattern more potent in strength. This then made it more energetically probable that future business opportunities at that particular property could experience similar problems.

We also have personal energy patterns resonating within our bio-auric fields that can keep us locked into repeating nonbeneficial patterns of behavior. Any energetic factor that aids in lowering the overall energy of a person, a business premises, a house, or a location will inhibit the optimal energetic flow, function, vitality, and success of all concerned. Think of a blanket being placed over a table lamp—the light is still there, yet the blanket significantly dims its glow! The blanket in this case being an energetic factor. Whether you are moving into a new home or business premises or you are having problems selling your home or you are having problems with the productivity and success of a business, you will be able to use the energy-clearing treatments found in part 3 of the book to greatly support you. Energy-clearing treatments work to restore spiritual and energetic balance and harmony back to a person, property, and business. They can also help rearrange the probable outcome of opportunities and new ventures to be in our favor. Why? Because we clear energetic resistance.

Furniture and Objects Hold Frequency

All things are composed of energy. Every material object is supported by its own specific energetic pattern that maintains its particular shape, design, and structural integrity. This includes the blueprint pattern of a property and all of the different materials required to build the property—bricks, plumbing, electrics, wood, the interior design, and all other individual things that come together to create a house. Since our thoughts, words, and feelings are also composed of energy, their electromagnetic charges can become absorbed into and attached onto the auric fields of furniture and physical objects, and even into the fabric (structure/substances) of the home. This is why an intuitive can place their hand on the wall of a home or even touch or hold a physical object in their hand, and they will be able to tune into the vibrations, energy patterns, and information resonating there. All objects also emit their own specific frequency or energy signature that makes them unique. Also, the energy frequency of the person who first invents, designs, and creates an object will also be imbued into the object's signature frequency. This is fine if, let's say, an item of furniture is designed with good intent and is made with the creative energies of love and joy. In this case, the creator of the furniture will naturally impress the furniture with beneficial energies. An object is an image that's been first held in the mind and has then become objectified. If, however, the item of furniture (or any object) was designed with a selfish intent and with the creative energy of greed, maybe through using less-than-efficient products to build it and not caring about its structural integrity and design, then the furniture in question will generate energy frequencies of greed, which significantly lowers its vibes. This clearly shows two very different kinds of creative intentions and energy frequencies that are set into the initial steps of one's own creations.

An item of furniture or any other object that carries such low vibes will emit its energetic signature directly into the home environment. In this sense, a specific area of the home can become less harmonious over time as it continuously radiates out its discordant energy field of its original creative intent. Energy vibrations can be measured through the process of a simple energy test (chapter 7) to check on the overall resonance. The good news is that energy fields of furniture and other objects can be easily cleared, which means there is no reason to discard anything that you love if they energy-tested as emitting low vibrational frequencies.

The objects within our home can originate from many different sources, time frames, and people. Some objects and items of furniture are inherited, and some are from antique stores. Other objects may come from a collection of our childhood things (possibly stored away in the garage, basement, or attic). Some objects may be due to a selection of wedding gifts, some loved and cherished and some not. Then there are those objects that are gifted to us, the ones we either keep on display because we love them or because the loved ones that bought them for us often visit our home and we don't wish to offend them.

Shove What You No Longer Love

Have you ever felt the desire to clear away all reminders of an ex-partner's presence in your home once the relationship ended? This is an intuitive desire to clear and break free of the energetic ties you once shared with each other. A releasing of their energies from your personal energies and from your home environment. This intuitive desire and process aids in the healing of any heartbreak and helps bring energetic closure to the relationship. Clearing away physical reminders of the relationship enables you to let go on many different levels of your being (physically, emotionally, mentally, and spiritually) so that you free the soul ties that once bound you to one another.

Sue broke up with her boyfriend of several years and was heartbroken. The romance ended due to her boyfriend cheating on her. In the process of accepting that the romance was finally over, Sue began to feel the need to clear away the physical reminders of their relationship, because looking at them kept the betrayal raw. A picture he'd painted her for her birthday hung on her bedroom wall. She would see it last thing at night before she went to sleep, which invoked mixed feelings of sadness and anger. Taking down the painting and then giving it away generated a feeling of great release. She replaced the empty space with a written sign that read "Inner Peace," which was the energy frequency her heart was seeking. Inner peace for her body and mind as she enters the sanctuary of her bedroom, and inner peace for her heart and soul to help her let go and heal.

Clearing away sentimental items may sound extreme to some people, who are quite happy to keep or store their possessions in the garage, basement, or loft for decades. Old cards and notes from previous partners may gather dust from a love long lost, while the person who wrote them has long since moved on. This reminds me of the very funny episode of the classic American comedy *Everybody Loves Raymond*, where Ray, a happily married man of three children, kept a recording of an ex-girlfriend breaking up with him during his school years, which was still stored away in his garage. On playing it back, it brought back all of his insecurities, which then began to cause problems in the present time and in his relationship with his wife, Deborah. Finally, he discards the recording and was immediately able to let go of the energetic ties to his past, and harmony was once again restored in the present.

Objects of our past can carry energetic reminders about the people and experiences associated with these objects that can trigger us emotionally in the present time. This is fine if we have great memories and we feel joyful when we connect to them. However, if these objects tend to invoke mixed feelings of sadness, regret, anger, hate, loss, grief, and any other emotional triggers from that time frame, and we purposely keep them hidden away because of this, then it makes sense to declutter and discard them mindfully. To be clear, I'm not talking about items that are dear to your heart that may have belonged to deceased family members and loved ones. My mom still uses her mom's beautiful dinner plates, still has her wedding ring, and often looks at many wonderful old photographs that invoke feelings of joy and sadness because she misses her due to the love they shared. This kind of sentimentality is fine because it is in harmony with unconditional love. What I'm talking about are the energetic ties that have no sincere or supportive emotional and spiritual connection to you.

Too many objects within the home can make the environment overly cluttered, and this can be energetically draining for us. Have you ever walked into a house or a room that's spilling over with clutter and you instantly felt overwhelmed? It's always a wise choice for you to "shove what you no longer love." By this statement, I don't mean to do so in a disrespectful manner, I just really like that saying! If you are giving something away to someone else, you could always energy-clear or bless the object first so that it's released with the energy of love. Energy-clearing treatments do not remove or clear any beneficial and supportive energies that may be held within an object or space, only the nonbeneficial kind. This is a win-win situation for you for anything that you personally clear in your home environment.

The less clutter you have in the home environment, the more harmonious the space and atmosphere become. This makes sense because of the interplay of all energies there and because excess clutter causes energy to stagnate. In removing excess clutter, you will naturally clear areas of stagnation so that life energy (chi) can flow around the home without restriction. The energy resonating within our home environment is also an extension and reflection of our consciousness, and by helping energy to flow more freely throughout the home, we will help support all aspects of our inner being. You've probably heard the phrase "A cluttered home is a cluttered mind." Keep any objects within your home that spark joy, since they will help generate a great atmosphere and create a harmonious environment.

CHAPTER 2

ENERGETIC RESIDUE

We shape our dwellings, and afterwards our dwellings shape us.
—WINSTON CHURCHILL

Twenty-One and Not Having Fun

I was frozen in terror and sat bolt upright in my chair as a mentally disturbed psychiatric patient in her late forties leaned over the reception desk toward me. I was twenty-one and the hairstylist at the psychiatric hospital's in-patient hair salon, and that particular day I was also alone since the other stylist was off sick. The patient glared straight at me with intense wild eyes mixed with an odd look of pleasure, since she could tell I was very afraid. She had happened to catch me off guard as I was counting the cash from the morning's takings, and I didn't notice her coming in. She immediately screamed and cursed at me, "Who the hell are you?"

The patient was standing in front of the only door and entrance/exit to the hair salon from the hospital's corridor and therefore blocked the only way out for me. My mind immediately raced for answers to how I could handle this situation, and all it could come up with was "This is exactly like a scary movie." Within seconds I knew that I was in real danger, since she noticed my hairdressing scissors lying upon the reception desk next to the appointment book. I knew I had to grab them before she did, and so we both went for them at the exact same time, and she won! My body's natural survival instinct kicked in as the mind attempted to quickly work out what my best options for safety were—fight or flight? With "my scissors" in "her hand," and held in the exact same position as the shower curtain scene from the movie *Psycho*, she began yelling over and over again: "I'm the devil; I'm the devil." In a nanosecond the thought "window" entered my mind, and I was up and running toward the only other possible way out for me without me having to directly confront her with scissors in hand. There in my favor was an open window located at the back of the salon.

I somehow managed to get myself through the half-open window, which lucky for me was located on the first floor, while she chased after me with my scissors held in the attack position. Thankfully, I landed on the grass and was instantly up and running as fast as I could as I headed for the hospital café that was situated next door. I burst in through their back door, which frightened the staff since I'd caught them off guard. I was finally safe. The staff in the café phoned for help. The patient was found, my scissors were carefully retrieved from her, and with the drama over, they returned her to her ward.

It was during this early period of my life that I learned firsthand knowledge from my daily experiences at the hospital about the dense, energetic atmosphere of my work environment. I spent a full year working at this hospital's hair salon, and my energy system was truly taxed and stressed as I came into daily contact with an array of low vibrational energies that were detrimental, extremely draining, and energetically toxic. My time spent within this hospital's work environment introduced me to a heavy blanket of emotional residue and trauma memories that vibrationally covered the hospital building, gardens, land, and even some of the surrounding area due to many decades of human suffering. I also became intuitively aware of what my childhood dreams had repeatedly revealed to me, as previously mentioned in the introduction, that ghosts and spirits were vibrationally connected to and drawn to the hospital's vibrational atmosphere and environment.

Ghosts and Spirits

Some patients at the hospital heard voices and received electric-shock treatment and heavy medication in order to attempt to stop this. Some of these voices originated from the ghosts and spirits vibrationally connected to the hospital building or attached to the people there. Ghosts can be described as picture imprints of etheric memories caught in the ether of earthly time. These imprints replay the same actions over and over. Consciousness is no longer active, since their soul essence has moved on to other realms within the Light. The ghostly picture is simply a captured visual memory, just like a short scene of a film. Sometimes the picture imprint will also include sounds, which is just noise imprinted within the ether and not originating from active consciousness. To give you an idea of ghostly imprints, think about the classic image of a beheaded man carrying his head as he wanders around the halls of an old castle. Other ghostly images caught in time appear at ancient battlegrounds and at old prisons such as Alcatraz, not forgetting those ghostly hitchhikers waiting for a ride at the side of a highway. I once saw a ghost crossing a road, and the image looked quite transparent yet unmistakably very human. There was no consciousness in the image or any way of communicating with the image; it was simply a memory still in play. Throughout the experience of time, these ghostly imprints eventually weaken and dissipate. The ghostly image seen crossing the road happened to be located at the site of many previous car and motorcycle accidents. The energetic residue left over from these accidents created a negative energy pattern of trauma within that particular area.

Not everyone will see ghosts, yet they may still register energetic responses through their nervous system if they happen to encounter one. Physical sensations of bodily shivers, feeling cold spots, and having goose bumps are signs that your nervous system is reacting to some kind of invisible residual energy, ghosts, or spirits. Residual trauma memories held within a space can lower the vibrational frequency resonating within that specific area, which then becomes an energetic disturbance. Clearing the residual emotional energy at such points of disturbance will help bring the energy back into greater balance, so that any negative energy patterns previously locked into the atmosphere there are either neutralized or removed. This will then make the area less of a hotspot for similar trauma to recur.

Earthbound Spirits

An earthbound spirit is a human soul who remains among the living instead of moving on to further realms of Light where they can continue on with the soul journey, evolution, and development. An earthbound spirit has consciousness and is therefore able to communicate to the living, unlike ghosts, which are images that are caught in time. Earthbound spirits haven't yet processed and cleared their energy fields, since they've yet to move into the realms of Light, which takes care of this. Until then, they will continue to carry their particular energy patterns and earthly desires with them, and they will still have the same level of consciousness they had while living. If they had any addictions while alive, such as to alcohol, sex, gambling, food, and drugs, then they will still desire these addictions because these energy patterns within their personal energies and consciousness are still active. They will then gravitate to those places and people of similar energetic resonance so that they can energetically attach to them in order to reexperience their human desires.

VISITING SPIRITS

There are also visiting spirits who have completely entered into the Light of a higher vibrational realm. Within the Light they've cleared the emotional residue of their previous life experience, have regained somewhat of an expanded consciousness, and are typically compassionate and understanding in nature. They able to revisit the earth plane and visit specific locations, loved ones, and friends and then return back to their rightful place in the realms of Light by their own free will. Reasons for their visitation can range from checking in on relatives, to bringing spiritual comfort and support to those in need, to assisting any souls who are ready to cross over. Some visiting spirits are classified as people's guides and guardian angels, and they visit us in this realm to perform specific tasks that include guidance and protection. There are also other benevolent Light beings such as guardian angels, angels assigned for different tasks, archangels, and other highly evolved souls who choose to assist humanity at this time. The psychiatric hospital environment was therefore a busy energetic mix of ghostly apparitions, earthbound spirits, visiting spirits, spirit guides, and angels.

Spirit Attachments

Earthbound spirits can attach their energy and consciousness to people, places, and objects through vibrational resonance. If an earthbound spirit attaches itself to a living human, the human host may or may not hear voices and may or may not feel a slight difference in character and personality. This is not what spirit possession is, which is very often misunderstood. The consciousness of the earthbound spirit can sometimes believe that the human host is actually its own physical body or its new physical body. In this sense they may feel they are reincarnating into a new body, which certainly doesn't happen in this way. While many spirit attachments aren't consciously bothersome to the human host, the attachment can keep the human host limited to some degree. This is because the host's energy field is being unwittingly depleted by the attachment, who requires an energy source to stay active.

If an earthbound spirit attaches to the energy patterns resonating within a property, the people living or working there may or may not become aware of its presence. Noises and even apparitions can be experienced within the property, and the atmosphere of the property can at times feel eerie and like we are being watched. If you are sensitive to the presence of an earthbound spirit within a property, you may sense atmospheric changes around you, and you may notice slight movements out of the corner of your eye. The overall vibration of the household or workplace can lower in frequency due to the paranormal activity encountered there. This kind of energetic disturbance can interfere with the personal energies of all those who spend time in that environment, including pets. A spirit attachment can also attach to an animal, an object, or an item of furniture. If someone lived in the house before you, and they loved the house so much that upon their death they didn't want to leave, then part of that person's soul energies can remain behind and earthbound. Secondhand jewelry, antiques, and inherited items may or may not have spirit attachments and residual energy absorbed into them from their previous owners.

Most spirit attachments have no evil intent and shouldn't be portrayed in the same way as Hollywood depicts demonic possession. They are typical human souls who—for whatever reason known to them—have remained within the atmosphere of the earth. Haunted homes are often due to spirit attachments. Spirit attachments also come with their own energetic residue, which includes any unhealed aspects or trauma memories, their death memory, and aspects of their personality, disposition, and character. When earthbound spirit attachments are energetically cleared and released to the Light, it immediately helps bring the overall energy of a person, place, or object back into greater vibrational harmony.

Paranormal Encounter

I was contacted by a young mother who claimed her house was haunted. Most of the time there are scientific reasons for the things that go bump in the night and for what many people assume is paranormal activity. The mother mentioned that her youngest child kept waking up at night crying and saying there was a man in her room. This in itself can simply be the result of a child having nightmares, yet other determining factors were also happening within the home that suggested that it could possibly be a spirit attachment issue. The mother explained there were also electrical problems, misplaced items, and children's toys that had moved location. Since energy-clearing treatments can be done from the comfort of our own home, with distance and location being no limitation, I didn't need to visit this young mom's home in order to help her. The young mother was located in the UK, and I was based in North Carolina, yet energy clearing has no bounds. From my own home I began an energy-clearing treatment of the young mom's home simply by using her full address as a point of my directed mental focus and intent, which then enabled me to spiritually and energetically reach the exact location. The spirit attachment was easily cleared and released to the Light. Residual energy and old energy patterns resonating within the home that initially attracted the earthbound spirit to the property were also cleared. The energy of the home environment immediately shifted and elevated. No further disturbances were reported, and the young child felt more settled. The atmosphere of the home felt lighter, brighter, and more homely.

Residual Energy

Being immersed in the emotional residual energy of the psychiatric hospital's environment five days a week energetically wiped me out. At twenty-one years old, and relatively fit and healthy, I should not have been so physically fatigued. Each night after work, it took all of the energy that I could physically muster just to have a bath, make my dinner, and go to bed. I kept wondering why I felt so tired when physically I was at my peak. Also, while I was asleep, I would experience night terrors. My yearlong experience working within the hospital's environment provided me with invaluable lessons about energetic residue and spirit attachments.

Feel the Vibes

Think about those times that you've energetically registered and intuitively felt the difference in the atmosphere of a room, building, someone's home environment, or your workplace. Maybe you've walked into a friend's home just after an argument has taken place, and you can feel the energetic tension still in the air. Maybe you've visited a so-called haunted location and you could sense and feel a change in the atmosphere due to some kind of energetic disturbance there. Suffering and destruction that's taken place within an environment will produce many inharmonious and discordant energies. Old battlegrounds, psychiatric hospitals, prisons, and places or homes that have experienced violence or murder can still contain residual trauma memories and emotional angst held within that etheric space. Some tangible physical signs of your nervous system registering such discordant energies can cause feelings of nausea and headaches since the energetic residue emanating there is not compatible with your own unique energetic signature.

House Memories

Every home contains house memories that carry energetic information about what has taken place there. House memories can be energetically cleared, which doesn't mean that the information about what happened there is wiped clean, since there will always be an etheric record of what has taken place. It simply means that in clearing the nonbeneficial energetic residue of any traumatic house memories, they will no longer negatively influence the space and the people living there. Some homes hold tragic house memories of traumatic events such as murder or suicide. In this case, energy-clearing work may need to be done more than once to help bring the home environment back into energetic harmony and balance.

Many people can't bring themselves to stay in a home after a tragedy has occurred there, due to the overwhelming emotional residue held within the atmosphere. Property can also be difficult to sell when tragedy has been experienced in the home, even when people are none the wiser about what trauma has previously taken place. The property radiates its sad message into the environment, which can also disturb the energetic balance of the surrounding area. Intuitively people can register this subtle information and stay clear of the home.

Often the places where horrific trauma has occurred are pulled down and destroyed, and memorials or flower gardens replace the property. There is much that can be done to help restore energetic harmony back to a home that has experienced trauma. When energetic harmony is restored within the home environment, it will also benefit the surrounding area and anyone who is energetically connected to the home. Heartfelt prayer directed to the location of such a horrific tragedy will help clear and transform the deeply imprinted emotional residue contained there. Leaving flowers outside the home as a form of condolence will help clear and elevate the space, since flowers emit high vibrational frequencies and healing qualities that can lighten the atmosphere. Flower essences do a similar thing for the human energy body when it's out of harmony. Each loving prayer directed to the home will all accumulate together to help vibrationally resolve the energetic disturbance. Memorials such as planted trees, flower gardens, statues, and a memorial service held at the spot will continue to help clear the energy there until a shift in balance eventually takes place, whereby the more dominant energy frequency becomes neutral or even positive. The time that this takes can vary depending on the severity of emotional energetic residue impregnated into the place. It really can take many years for deeply imprinted trauma energies to become more neutral to the environment or to shift to positive energy. Energetic residue will clear layer by layer in such traumatic cases until the originating charge is finally neutralized.

Land Memory

When you think about how many generations of people have lived before you, and what may have previously existed upon the land where your home is now built, we enter into the fascinating realm of land memories. This is what the James Hutton Institute[2] has to say about land memory, whose vision is to be at the forefront of innovative and transformative science for sustainable management of land, crop, and natural resources that supports thriving communities.

Soil is the memory of the land. Sounds odd or a little New Age? Let's explain. Soils, like people, are the product of both their genetic material and their environment. For people, the genetic material is our DNA. For soil, it is the rock, sediment, or other geological material that soil is built up from. The environment includes a number of factors such as climate, flora and fauna, and topography that produce the soil's character over time. Soils therefore carry a history, often thousands of years long, within them, and this history can be read and understood by those with the skills and experience to do so. So, when we say that soil is the memory of the land, it is because all of the things that have happened to the land over time are recorded, minutely or in broad strokes, within the soil.

This history recorded within the soil also includes the history of any residual trauma energies and memories. If some kind of emotional trauma and human suffering has taken place upon the land, then the earth energy in that place will resonate the traumatic emotional residue deep within the ground. This disturbance can then lower the vibrational resonance of the land, including the ground that's directly located underneath a property. In adversely affecting the energy of the land, any crops that may have been planted there can have problems growing because of the inhospitable environment for flora, fauna, and other aspects of nature.

There is an innate spiritual intelligence operating behind nature that can help restore the optimal conditions for the land and for flourishing flora and fauna. In Findhorn, Scotland, Peter and Eileen Caddy, along with Dorothy Maclean, unintentionally founded the Findhorn community in 1962.[3] All three had dedicated themselves to following a disciplined spiritual path for many years. When times became difficult and with little money, they moved to a caravan park in the nearby costal village of Findhorn. Peter decided to grow vegetables, and although the land there was sandy and dry, he persevered. In her mediation, Dorothy discovered she was able to intuitively contact the overseeing intelligence of plants, which she called angels, and then devas, who gave her instructions on how to make the most of their fledgling garden. They placed this guidance into action with amazing results. In the barren sandy soil of Findhorn Bay Caravan Park, they grew huge plants, herbs, and flowers, most famously the now-legendary 40-pound cabbages. Word spread and horticultural experts came and were stunned, and the garden at Findhorn became famous.

If the land you live upon has emotional energetic residue or is inhospitable in some way that you are unable to take care of your garden in the way that you desire, then you can connect with the spiritual intelligence of the land to support you. The spirit of the land is known as the guardian and nature spirit of the place. With their spiritual cocreative assistance, the land can receive the necessary energetic frequencies that can help restore vital balance to support the nurturing of the land and the well-being of the property upon the land and all who live there.

The tangible results of doing an energy-clearing treatment of any traumatic land memories can be observed in the look and feel of the land. For those with crops, they will see them flourish, and for those who plant flowers, they will see them bloom. Nature will return with an abundant life force, and the birds will be drawn back to the area. The property upon the land will receive beneficial foundational support that can help maintain the structural integrity of the place. While general care and maintenance of a property are always going to be required to keep the property in good working order, if the energy vibration of the land and property is in harmony with beneficial energies, then there will be much less likelihood of major structural problems or disasters such as fire, flooding, and roof damage.

CHAPTER 3:

ENERGETIC INTERFERENCE

Poisons are not necessarily that which you may consume through food. Poisons can enter you in so many ways: a wrong thought, a wrong emotion, a wrong idea, wrong energy, or a wrong impulse can poison your life.

—SADHGURU

Why Do I Feel So Strange?

Energetic interference is any kind of energy that's not compatible with our own energy system and therefore causes us to have some kind of adverse reaction to it, from mild to major. Fatigue, feeling nauseated and dizzy, feeling anxious, and generally feeling out of sorts are just some of the symptoms of energetic interference. Numerous sources, factors, and forces can be responsible for energetic interference, such as geopathic stress, technological overload, astrological influences, and even the energies of other people.

Energetic interference affects our personal energy fields and the energy resonance of our home or work environment. It can interfere with our immune system responses, our vital health, our memory and concentration, and the productivity of our day. In the workplace, lack of productivity will interfere with the business and our creativity. Energetic interference can also cause problems in the relationships between employees and customers. In the household, lack of productivity will interfere with taking care of the daily requirements and, as such, things can quickly become messy, making us feel even more overwhelmed with our list of chores. When we understand more about energetic interference, then we can take charge of the situation and begin to transform it so that we can keep potential issues at bay.

Technological Overload

Technological overload can cause havoc with our energy systems. We can become stressed by the electromagnetic fields radiating within our home or work environment, otherwise known as EMFs. These electrical fields of current can adversely affect people, and their nonbeneficial reactions to these fields will depend solely on their sensitivity and receptivity to them. If someone is already experiencing excess stress, then their personal energies will be weaker, and they can potentially become more vulnerable to the negative effects of EMFs.

It's true that some people aren't affected at all by EMFs, and yet for others it can be very debilitating. My thoughts about this are that it can depend on the amount of EMFs radiating within a person's space, plus how long a person has been continuously exposed to them and how well balanced their energy system is. As recently mentioned, an already stressed system due to excess stress will be more compromised.

It's quite impossible to live in an EMF-free environment if we want to use all of the useful benefits that come with advanced technology, such as cell phones, computers, Wi-Fi, and other appliances and devices that make our lives easier. What we can do is to help our personal energy fields become more able to cope with, harmonize, and adapt to these EMFs. As technology continues to advance and evolve, our own systems will eventually learn to adapt and evolve in harmony with our environment, so that we may enjoy the life that we are creatively a part of. We can learn to thrive in a sea of energies so that we have greater immunity to such adverse energetic interference.

We are living in an advanced technological age, and while many folks do not want to advance in this way, the majority of the collective consciousness of humanity does; otherwise it would not unfold in this particular way. Conspiracy theories also abound over the new leaps in technology, and some may even be true, because we do live in a world of duality and not everything is intended for our greater good. However, we also have the creative ability to take charge of our energy systems so that we don't have to suffer the detrimental effects. So, while an energy-clearing treatment won't remove the EMF, it can certainly help clear and reduce the harmful effects of the EMF on our systems and within our homes and workplace so that we become more neutral to them. By identifying and clearing the energy of the EMFs in your home or workspace, you will help support your immunity to them so that your health stays balanced, plus you will empower your nervous system and brain health so that you can focus, concentrate, and remember things more clearly. Clearing the energy of EMFs in the workplace will help support the health and well-being of the staff. Here's a look at some of the possible EMF interference that can be found within our home or work environments.

Possible EMF Interference

Wi-FI
Cable
Computers/devices
Cell phone / cordless phone
Electrical wiring
Gas or water main
Smart TV
Microwave oven
Kitchen appliances
Artificial lighting
Hairdryer/straightener/other

I once heard a story about a young boy who had constant buzzing in his ears. He told his mom it sounded as though he had a bee's nest in his head. His mom took him to see a doctor, who couldn't find anything wrong to explain the buzzing noise. The mom then reached out to an expert dowser, who through a process of energy diagnostic work was able to discern that the cordless telephone was the culprit. The mom turned off the cordless phone and didn't mention it to her son, to see if anything would happen. Within twenty minutes the boy told his mom the buzzing in his head had gone. This is how sensitive the boy was to the energy frequency of the cordless phone, yet others in the household were totally immune to it. We all have unique energetic signatures, and our energy fields fluctuate in strength or weakness according to our moods and to any trauma or shock we've experienced or are currently experiencing. We may become affected by EMFs at some point in our lives only to overcome their interference when our energy systems rebalance.

Geopathic Stress (Earth Energies)

Geopathic stress creates harmful earth energies and is considered to be another invisible detrimental energy factor that can potentially cause us health problems. While there are various types of earth energies, and some that are beneficial for us, geopathic stress energies emit vibrations that interfere with the human body, typically lowering a person's immunity, which makes it more difficult for them to overcome disease.

Feng shui masters have developed a great understanding of these earth energies, and they apply this knowledge when siting a building to locate the most favorable spot, and to determine which areas to avoid. Old European traditions still describe scenarios where a herd of sheep was observed before a house was built. The spot where the sheep bedded down for the night would be the best area, specifically for the master bedroom, since it was free of geopathic stress. The first notable study in recent history was conducted by Gustav Freiherr von Pohl,[4] a German aristocrat, in 1929. Freiherr von Pohl conducted an experiment where he dowsed a whole small town, Vilsbiburg, for geopathic stress. He was accompanied by a policeman to ensure that he did not ask questions of the town's inhabitants. The results were then taken to the town mayor, who compared the results with the town's doctor's records of patients with cancer over the previous several years. The results produced a 100 percent correlation between cancer and geopathic stress. The experience was repeated in larger and smaller towns, always with the same results—100 percent correlation. Gustav Freiherr von Pohl's book *Earth Currents—Causative Factor of Cancer and Other Diseases* was published in Munich in 1932.[5] While there are many factors that can cause, contribute to, and predispose a person to develop cancer, the study and experiment done by Gustav Freiherr von Pohl are of great importance for further scientific research into the matter of nonbeneficial earth energies and their correlation to disease, or at the very least to them weakening a person's immunity to disease.

Geo means "earth" and *pathic* means "suffering," so geopathic stress represents earth stress. Geopathic stress occurs when the earth's magnetic field is disturbed. Natural ways in which this happens are due to underground fault lines and subterranean water veins and currents that emit harmful electromagnetic fields. When these stressed earth energies run directly under our home or workplace, then potential health issues can be a factor. Planet Earth also has its own energetic grid that carries vital energies throughout the planet. Energy runs along these grid pathways, which have been called earth meridians. When these earth meridians become overly stressed due to changes in the earth's magnetic field and other factors, then they will begin to radiate stressed detrimental energy upward into the environment. If our home happens to be located above any geopathic stress, then we may experience a potential health hazard. Another cause of geopathic stress is due to shock waves rippling beneath the earth from building upon the surface and digging deep into the ground for structural stability and installing pipelines and wires. This often causes a disturbance with the way that energy flows as it responds to what's happening within the ground. When a lot of building work takes place, it stresses the surface area, the surrounding land, and the ground beneath the buildings. Whenever energy is disturbed in some way, it shifts the equilibrium of life force by changing it into unhealthful and erratic energy patterns that radiate its frequencies outward as well as upward into the environment above the ground. If you live in a home that has two or three floors, or your business is located several floors high, you can still be affected by nonbeneficial earth energies as they get transmitted upward. It's not just the ground floor that's affected, as some might think, because of its orientation with the earth.

Underground water can conduct electricity, and because our thoughts and emotions leave electrical charges in the atmosphere and environment, these underground streams can become adversely affected by humanity's suffering and discordant thinking as energy moves upon matter. The water absorbs the nonbeneficial energy and carries the information along its flow. For example, any underground streams flowing beneath the psychiatric hospital where I once worked would be adversely affected by an accumulation of negative human thought forms and the emotional suffering taking place there. This would cause an imbalance within the natural elements of the water, and its equilibrium would shift. Discordant energy will then be carried along its intended flow all around the surrounding area, transmitting energetic interference along its path.

Geopathic stress can be more prominent in different areas of the home. If there is an area of geopathic stress found directly under the bed, for instance, then it can disturb the sleep patterns of whoever sleeps there, even contributing to chronic insomnia. If there is any area of geopathic stress within your office, it can cause an energetic shift in your bio-auric field and nervous system. Lack of concentration, a foggy mind, and feeling drained and anxious can then result.

THE SURROUNDING AREA

The local area surrounding our home or place of work can at times have an adverse energetic effect on our environment if there is some kind of energetic disturbance radiating its nonbeneficial energies toward our location. It's true that we often don't know what goes on behind the closed doors of our neighbors or local businesses. While the majority of people will be decent folk, there will be those who are less conscious of their actions and of the discordant creative energy they express directly into the atmosphere. Violence, abuse, and any emotional and mental control going on behind someone's closed doors will disturb the energy of that property, plus it can adversely affect the energy of the surrounding area and neighborhood. Other factors that can disturb the energetic balance of the surrounding area are things such as crime and accidents. If the overall energy vibration of the surrounding area where you live or work drops significantly in vibration, then it can become a hotbed for further trouble due to the frequency range it's broadcasting. Energetic resonance will draw to it that of like vibration and further crime, and problems may then continue. If you enter a neighborhood that's crime ridden, you may feel the energy of the area as being dense, heavy, toxic, chaotic. Physically, at times your own energy system may respond to low vibrational energy with a shiver. The reason why your body shivers is that it's a natural reaction for you to shake off the negative energy.

Accidents, especially traffic accidents, also create an energetic disturbance within the surrounding area that will radiate discordant energy fields out to the surrounding area. A traffic accident will emit the heightened chaotic energy frequencies of fear, trauma, and shock, plus the energy that's created from the actual impact itself. All of this can disturb the energetic harmony of the surrounding area where your property or place of work may be located.

Cosmic Influence
(Astrological Influence and Radiation)

If you are fascinated by astrology, then you've no doubt heard about the adverse effects of Mercury retrograde, when the effects of that planet can directly influence the earth's atmosphere and the personal energy fields and consciousness of people, animals, and nature. When the moon enters different phases, it also broadcasts different frequencies that align with these phases, and they will influence the atmosphere of the planet, people, tides, water, and animals. This kind of nonbeneficial influence can create emotional outbursts, crime can rise, accidents can increase, and our attitude and behavior can alter. All of these discordant influences can be energetically cleared so that you remain balanced when the energy around you is a little chaotic. Yet, just like there are nonbeneficial cosmic influences, there are also an incredible array of beneficial ones that emanate from the celestial realm and stream down as divine light frequencies into the earth's atmosphere. These divine light frequencies carry angelic consciousness, divine attributes, and extraordinary creative power. They are responsible for clearing areas of the planet, as well as aiding in the healing regeneration of people, animals, and nature.

Other People's Energies

Have you ever noticed that when you spend time with people who complain a lot that you begin to feel the need to detach from their conversation and their energy field? This is because unless you are able to rise above their constant complaints, your own energy system will start reacting to the low vibration they are giving out. If you've had a long day and are mentally tired, or maybe you are physically fatigued from work or you are run down because of a cold, then your own energy system will become more vulnerable to energetic interference. If you listen to your intuitive guidance system and make your excuses and leave, then you will no doubt save yourself from experiencing further energetic drain. If your energy is balanced and you are strong and energized, it's less likely that you will become compromised by the energetic interference of others. In rising above people's complaints, you may even be able to positively influence them to do the same. People who don't desire to become more positive will, however, not respond to your positive influence and will continue to complain. The electromagnetic energy charge of what they complain about will remain within their bio-auric fields so that they will continue to attract more things to complain about. What we are grateful for and we bless will help clear our energetic stress so that our bio-auric fields of light help us attract and create more-beneficial experiences and opportunities.

Negative-Focused Thought

People can also adversely affect our energy systems through their focused negative thoughts. Our negative thoughts and feelings about a person can also interfere with that person's energy, even when we don't deliberately wish them any harm.

Thoughts have creative power, and even gossiping harshly about someone is enough to adversely affect that person's energies, moods, and behavior. Participating in negative thoughts, opinions, and judgments about ourselves and others will weaken our own vibrational resonance and will limit our creative power. Our personal dreams and heartfelt goals often require a lot of creative power to be able to bring them into reality. A low vibrational frequency weakens a person's attractor and creator fields of power, thereby interfering with the manifestation of their personal goals. People unwittingly block the universal flow of good that truly wants to come to them because of their secret negative thoughts. If a person's consciousness and energy fields are high vibe enough, the negative effects of other people's energy will be less effective on them. This is because the clearer our energy system, consciousness, and fields are, the stronger the Light within us becomes. This Light is the spark of our Spirit, which transmutes all lesser vibrational frequencies either intentionally or unintentionally directed to us. A Clear Spirit is the path to unlimited creative power, health, harmony, abundance, and joy. Each chapter of this book is designed toward you creating this outcome!

NEGATIVE INTENT/CURSES

Throughout the ages a negative intent that's directed toward someone, something, some piece of land, or some property has been labeled as curse energy. Both curses and blessings are mentioned in the Bible, and many theologians and professionals have researched this subject. Medical doctor Larry Dossey has researched and goes into great detail about the power of prayer in several of his bestselling books, in which he mentions that there are benevolent prayers that carry light and what he terms negative prayers, sometimes called black prayer, that are in alignment with dark energies/forces. In black prayer, physician Dossey states that rather than asking the Absolute to intercede benevolently in human affairs, one invokes destructive powers with the intent to harm or cause havoc. In Dossey's bestselling book *Healing Words: The Power of Prayer and the Practice of Medicine*,[6] he includes the following story about negative influences in the laboratory. I include it here to give you an idea of how destructive negative intent can adversely affect living organisms.

Olgar Worrall: "I Refuse to Hurt Them"[7]

Many healers who use prayer power to help others will freely admit its potential for harm. Among them was the late Olga Worrall, the well-known psychic healer. Beverly Rubik, director of the Center of Frontier Sciences at Temple University, and physicist Elizabeth Rauscher performed laboratory studies on Worrall, whose approach to healing was deeply spiritual and grounded in prayer. Rubik asked Worrall to interact with a suspension of bacteria, inhibiting or retarding their growth or actually killing them. Bacterial counts would then be made and compared to a control sample. Rubik could then determine with great accuracy whether Worrall could exert a real effect or not on living organisms. Worrall strenuously objected. "I refuse to hurt them," she said. "I will only use my abilities for good." Honoring her wishes, Rubik modified the experiment in a way that enabled Worrall to use her powers positively. Two samples of bacteria would be exposed to the toxic effects of an antibacterial agent, and Worrall would "protect" one sample but not the other. The results showed that the "protected" bacteria indeed survived in greater numbers than the controls, at levels of great statistical significance.

— Larry Dossey, *Healing Words: The Power of Prayer and the Practice of Medicine* (New York. HarperOne, 1995)[8]

This important result provides evidence that through the power of positive, focused, and directed thought, and through the concept of the "One Mind" connection that we share with all reality, we really do have the ability to intervene and help others with thoughts of love, healing, and protection. It also shows that the opposite intent is sadly true—a destructive negative intent is capable of being directed to any living organism or object, situation, property, and land. This is because we live in a world of duality and we have free-will expression that we share with a diversity of human consciousness, ranging from misguided minds to those minds who are full of light. Those people who do choose to intentionally harm others, no matter how justified they feel they are, will by universal law incur karmic return. What they dish out energetically to others, they will also receive back energetically in ways that will keep them from evolving until they begin to reconnect once more with their heart energy. Until then, they become a prime candidate for a variety of life lessons.

As well as independent scientific studies for such thought power phenomena, there have also been government studies on the use of mind control. A selection of experts (those who had developed the power of a focused mind) were asked to use their intent and thought power to stop a pig's heart. The Hollywood film *The Men Who Stare at Goats* was based on this.[9]

CHAPTER 4

PERSONAL ATMOSPHERE

Everyone should consider his body as a priceless gift from one whom he loves above all, a marvelous work of art, of indescribable beauty, and mystery beyond human conception, and so delicate that a word, a breath, a look, nay, a thought may injure it.

—Nikola Tesla

We Are Spiritual and Energetic Beings

While we all understand the importance of taking care of our physical body's needs, fewer of us understand the importance of taking care of our energy needs. We don't think twice about taking a shower to wash away the dirt and debris of the day, yet we need to consider that our energies also contain energetic grime that would benefit from a daily or weekly energy clearing. By taking care of our basic energetic requirements, we engage in an innate form of preventive medicine. Looking after our personal energies can help support the health and well-being of our physical body. When our energies are clear, coherent, and in greater energetic balance, we will naturally amplify our vital energy levels. We will also help magnify our soul's creative power to attract and create our personal goals and heartfelt dreams into physical reality. When our energies are slow, incoherent, and imbalanced, we unwittingly weaken our vital energy levels, and we interfere with and limit our soul's creative power. Our creative power transmits a specific frequency that generates a vibrational force field of magnetic light within and around us. If we emit a weakened vibrational force field of light, then we are limited in what we can attract and create in our lives because we simply lack the necessary energy and creative power to do so. The good news is that we can shift our vibrational resonance at any time that we consciously decide to raise our vibes. Our thoughts, beliefs, attitudes, and emotions are what greatly influence our vibrational resonance. Our mind energy is superpowerful, and it directly affects our physical health and well-being. You've probably heard the term "mind over matter," and since our physical body consists of dense matter, then we can positively influence our body's energies with our mind's extraordinary creative power. Our creative mind becomes expansive and unlimited when we join as one creative force with the divine mind and universal intelligence. Let's read what some remarkable metaphysical, spiritual, and scientific men and women of the world say about our personal energies and the power of our creative mind.

Albert Einstein: "Matter is energy. Energy is Light. We are all Light Beings."

Joseph Murphy: "All disease originates in the mind. Nothing appears on the body unless there is a mental pattern corresponding to it."

Paramahansa Yogananda: "Thought is the primary energy and vibration that emanated from God and is thus the creator of life, electrons, atoms, and all forms of energy."

Florence Scovel Shinn: "Words and thoughts are a tremendous vibratory force ever molding man's body and affairs."

Charles Fillmore: "Let the God within you express itself through you in the world without."

Helena Petrovna Blavatsky: "The Universe is worked and guided from within outwards."

Phineas Parkhurst Quimby: "The trouble is in the mind, for the body is only the house for the mind to dwell in. If your mind has been deceived by some invisible enemy into a belief, you have put it into the form of a disease, with or without your knowledge. By my theory or truth, I come in contact with your enemy and restore you to health and happiness."

Catherine Ponder: "That your words have unlimited power has been a truth known since ancient times. Primitive man used affirmations through incantation. When there was a healing need, the priest–medicine man was called to speak words of healing."

In reading these enlightening quotes about energy, mind, and thought, we gain the understanding and awareness that energy follows thought, and we can change our thoughts and transform our personal energies at any time. This important factor means that we are able to consciously direct energy through setting specific mental intentions that will begin to make subtle to significant transformational shifts occur within our consciousness, within our physical body, and within our life experience. Just like what Florence Scovel Shinn stated when she said that "words and thoughts are a tremendous vibratory force ever molding man's body and affairs." Our outer environment and life experiences offer a direct reflection back to us about the quality of our consciousness. If we want to transform our environment and our health and improve our life experiences, then we must first make conscious beneficial changes within our consciousness.

Our Spiritual and Energetic Anatomy

Each one of us has a spiritual and energetic anatomy in the same way that we have a physical body anatomy. When our physical body is sick, it's already been programmed by its divine designer to repattern, regenerate, and heal itself—to move back to what the medical world terms *homeostasis*. This repatterning is always done on an energetic level first in one of our bio-auric energy bodies to help restore energetic equilibrium. Our spiritual and energetic anatomy includes several energy bodies, with their seven bio-auric fields of light, twelve energy meridians (with two additional ones that carry vital energy around our body), and energy centers known as chakras, which are portals of light and energy power stations for the physical and subtle energy bodies. We also have feminine and masculine polarities and the five elements of nature, which include earth energy, water energy, fire energy, air energy, and space/etheric energy. Each element is responsible for different structures and functions in the human body. For the purpose of doing a personal energy-clearing treatment for yourself or others, I include information in this chapter only about our seven energy bodies and our seven main chakras because these are more than sufficient to work with in order to reach every aspect of our body, emotions, mind, and Spirit.

Our Spirit aspect also contains our spiritual DNA, of our true divine cosmic nature. It is who we truly are, and it always reflects perfect love and unlimited creativity. Our Spirit is the eternal aspect of us that is already evolved and is One with the Creator, the Universe, and all other Spirits. Our soul is the vehicle that journeys through the dimensions of Light and matter while empowered by the spark of our Spirit so that we can have a physical life experience. Our soul contains records of our soul history of every experience we've ever had in this life, other lives, other dimensions, other universes, and other timelines. As eternal Spirit beings we don't just have the one life, which makes no cosmic sense at all. Let's now explore a little more of our energy bodies and energy centers.

Our Energy Bodies and Auric Fields

First Energy Body/Field: The Etheric Body

The first energy body is known as the etheric body. Its energetic pattern and design interpenetrate with the physical body as well as surrounding the body in a field of light. The etheric energy body is the exact replica of the physical body, which creates the foundation for its physical form. It provides and maintains the structural integrity of the body's organs, systems, and parts. Our dense physical body is the end result of all the energy bodies interpenetrating and supporting each other, while the etheric body serves as the energetic matrix for our cellular growth. If you think of what an architect's blueprint looks like for a proposed house plan, you will get an insight into what the etheric body looks like. It is a human body pattern made up of many intricate energy lines that crisscross all over the body to form an amazing grid work and map of our physical form. This remarkable grid work is responsible for how cellular growth takes place and how the tissues of the body are formulated into their specific intended designs. An etheric energy pattern for the liver will have a different blueprint design to the etheric energy pattern for the heart or lungs. Each etheric pattern will also have its own unique vibrational frequency, and if the physical dense counterpart remains on its correct vibrational frequency, then the integrity of the organ in question remains vitally intact and does the job it's designed to do. If the vibrational frequency alters and shifts off its intended energy frequency, then dysfunction with the physical organ can set in because its primary resonance has changed. The organ in question will no longer have the correct energetic support to keep it vitally sustained, and therefore malfunction can set in. Such problems with the organ may also cause a physical disturbance with the associated body system or body part that it's directly connected with.

The etheric energy body is perfect in its original divine design, yet certain factors do interfere with its structural integrity. These factors include both our physical DNA and spiritual imbalances from our soul history. Faulty genetics originating from our ancestor timeline or some kind of trauma memory originating from our soul history timeline can create a disturbance in its perfect blueprint pattern. This disturbance causes an energetic distortion within the grid work of the etheric body, from which the physical body is formed. The disturbance is then projected as a dysfunction or problem of the physical body.

If the physical body is compromised due to some injury, then this physical disturbance is also reflected into the etheric body. The etheric lines of light behind the body part that is injured or amputated can become fractured or scrambled, which then causes energetic imbalances within the etheric body. Environmental factors such as toxins and poisons that adversely affect the equilibrium of the physical body will also cause an energetic imbalance within the etheric energy body. Rather than causing any broken lines of etheric light such as with an injury, the imbalance typically affects the overall resonance of the etheric body so that it's moved off its optimal energetic frequency and function. This means that its cellular support for the regeneration process of the physical body is slowed down or weakened, and the physical body can then take longer to heal until energetic harmony is restored. In the case of physical factors and environmental toxins causing such a disturbance within the etheric body, medical assistance and medication can help restore homeostasis to the physical body, which will then restore harmony to the etheric body to continue to help the body regenerate. If illness or disease is due to the manifested effects of emotional trauma, shock, and other psychological or spiritual factors, then it is the etheric body that first becomes disturbed through the imbalances resonating in the other energy bodies (the emotional, mental, and spiritual bodies). The etheric body will then project its imbalances into the psychical body, which then results in physical malfunction in some way.

Energy-clearing treatments can help clear and correct these energetic disturbances at the etheric body level before they have a chance to take root in the physical body. If we already have persisting health issues, aches, and pains from old injuries, and physical trauma and shock from any surgery we've encountered, then doing an energy clearing of our etheric body can bring some relief and at times even improvements or total resolution of these issues. Because our etheric body is also influenced by our genetic inheritance and our soul history energy through its cellular memory, an energy clearing of the etheric body can help clear the adverse energetic effects of any ancestor trauma memories and past-life or prelife trauma memories upon us. This can help us become less predisposed to any probable genetic inheritance problems and can improve or resolve any spiritual problems. Once cleared and resolved, they will no longer adversely affect us and future generations.

Second Energy Body/Field: The Emotional Body

Our second energy body is called the emotional body, which is associated with our emotional health and well-being. Its energetic constitution is much finer than the etheric body, which gives it a faster vibrational frequency. It follows, surrounds, and interpenetrates the shape and outline of the etheric body and therefore provides emotional information to the etheric body. Information is passed down from the higher energy bodies of light to the ones directly below them. The mental body, for example, is the next energy body of light that's more refined in vibrational frequency than the emotional body. It interpenetrates and communicates with the emotional body below it, as well as communicating with the astral energy body that's vibrationally above it. The mental body provides information about our state of mind to the emotional body that if imbalanced in some way will then cause a disturbance in the emotional body. A disturbance within the emotional body, if not cleared or resolved, can then cause a disturbance within the etheric body, which can then eventually move into the dense physical body to manifest as a physical complaint.

Our emotional body, as its name suggests, directly deals with our feelings and emotions. Each emotion we have emits a specific frequency and color resonance. Our emotions and feelings generate an array of colors within the emotional body's energy field that change in tone and shape depending on our moods and our overall emotional balance. When we feel emotionally balanced, we will project softened energy clouds of pastel colors. When we are emotionally imbalanced, we project darker tones of color that can also merge together to create denser blobs of energy. These blobs of pulsating energy tend to gravitate down to the next denser energy body, which in this case would be the etheric body. If a person is very angry and in the heat of an argument, then not only will the emotional outburst move down into the etheric body, which can then trigger tears in the physical body or some other kind of physical reaction, but it will also emerge into the atmosphere as an energetic charge and create an emotional reaction within the environment.

A client of mine emailed me about having a very sore neck. She had seen a chiropractor and had used pain relief gel on her neck and shoulders, yet the complaint still persisted. Typically, if pain persists when medical intervention is unable to alleviate it, then there will be an emotional imbalance tied to the pain that needs to be either processed, cleared, or resolved. An energy clearing of her etheric body in the area of her neck (etheric neck) along with a clearing of her emotional body (anger, worry, fear energy) helped correct the imbalance. Within twenty-four hours the pain in her neck was gone, and she also felt more emotionally balanced.

Third Energy Body/Field: The Mental Body

Our third energy body is called the mental body, which is associated with our mental health and well-being. Its constitution is of a finer substance and vibration than the emotional body below it. The mental energy body typically illuminates around our head and shoulders as a glowing field of golden-yellow light, yet it also extends around the whole body. Our thought processes, attitude, knowledge, beliefs, and mental pictures create energy patterns within the mental energy body. Positive energy patterns help develop our personal power, increase our confidence, and support our overall consciousness. Limiting energy patterns due to negative thoughts or beliefs, a bad attitude, or fearful mental pictures, images, and visions generates imbalances and congestion within our mental body. Limiting energy patterns interfere with the quality of our consciousness and our personal and creative power.

Our intellect and the way we analyze ourselves, others, and the world all impact the energy vibration of our mental body. A tired mind is often the result of overthinking and overanalyzing, which creates energetic congestion within the mental body that can create a fog-like appearance around the head and shoulders. If this energy then gravitates down through the emotional body to the etheric body and then into the physical body, headaches, foggy-mindedness, and nervous tension can result. Our dominant thoughts and feelings also create thought forms within our mental body. These thought forms look like blobs of light that carry intelligence. Each thought form will have its own emotional trigger because our mental body interpenetrates with our emotional body below it.

As we experience different life challenges, gaining awareness and knowledge, and we evolve our consciousness, we also help restructure and expand our mental energy body. Old energy patterns are broken down and new ones are formulated. Our level of willpower, decision-making, ego mind, intellect, and discernment create vibrational shifts within our mental body. Other people's thoughts and influence can also affect the energy vibration of our mental body. The belief systems of our heritage, culture, and environment can also influence our mental body. What we have accepted as being true for us becomes part of our mental makeup. Our mental freedom arises from our personal power when we begin to examine old belief systems that no longer serve our growth, and so we willingly choose more-appropriate ones. In letting go of limited patterns, we overcome our mental limitations and we restore our personal power. When we are in greater mental balance and equilibrium, we are able to think more clearly, become more decisive in decision-making, have clearer discernment, and gain stronger willpower to break through unhealthful patterns and habits of behavior. A mental energy body clearing can feel like a breath of fresh air due to easing nervous tension from a congested mind. It can help calm the nerves and generate optimism since we think and feel lighter and brighter in thought and emotion.

Fourth Energy Body/Field: The Astral Body (Heart/Soul Body)

Our fourth energy body is known as the astral body. It's where the magic of our heart and soul energies can be found. The astral body is the energy bridge between the physical realm and the heaven realms (or spirit realms). When we are in greater alignment with our heart and soul energies, we will create our life experiences from a place of love and not fear. Whenever we are in touch with and express the energies of compassion, kindness, empathy, and unconditional love, this will help expand our heart and soul energy and elevate our overall vibrational frequency. Our astral body is influenced by our traumas and heartache, and so many of our trauma memories are stored there. These trauma memories generate powerful fields of resistance that form around the heart and soul energies that can limit us. They work as a form of self-protection to prevent us from opening our heart again and trusting in others in case we get deeply hurt. While they may do well to protect us, they are also in alignment with fear energy and not love, which means they can prevent us from living fully from our heart and experiencing greater joy. These energetic fields of resistance also limit our soul's creative power, and we tend to create from a place of fear, which blocks the manifestation of our heartfelt dreams and desires. An energy clearing of the astral body can help dissolve these trauma fields of resistance so that our heart and soul energies are able to fully engage in all aspects of life.

Fifth Energy Body/Field: The Spiritual–Pattern Body

Our fifth energy body is the spiritual-pattern body or template body. Its structure and design formulate a spiritual blueprint pattern for the first energy body (the etheric body). The spiritual-pattern body is the perfect design and form for the etheric energy body to replicate. It acts as a cosmic map for the etheric body to create the physical body. When there is dysfunction in the etheric body due to hereditary factors, trauma energies, and injuries, an energy-clearing treatment can help the spiritual-pattern body communicate its perfect pattern to the etheric body so that repairs can take place. The perfect nature of the spiritual-pattern body works to project its intelligence into the etheric body so that energetic shifts and changes take place. Astonishing healing results can take place simply from helping all of our energy bodies to support each other as they are designed to prior to any energetic resistance and interference.

Sixth Energy Body/Field: The Cosmic Body

Our sixth energy body is the cosmic body or celestial body. Our cosmic body is fluid in nature and of a cosmic substance that's much finer in vibrational resonance than all the energy bodies below it. It's spiritually perceived as a shimmering light body—think of the twinkling of stars with golden and silver light. Other beautiful colors of rainbow light in their palest form are also perceived within this extraordinary cosmic body. Our cosmic body enables our soul to expand our consciousness beyond the physical realm to be open to receive divine inspiration, ideas, and insight. Whenever we pray or meditate, our cosmic body becomes brighter and aligns us with divine intelligence. This unlimited process enables us to cocreate our lives with universal support, spiritual guidance, and surrender. An energy clearing of the cosmic body can help us align our consciousness with universal abundance so that we can manifest from an unlimited perspective. Our cosmic body enables us to feel a deep spiritual connection with the universe and with each other.

Seventh Energy Body/Field: The Causal Body

Our seventh energy body is the causal body, which is associated with our innate spiritual nature and heritage. This extraordinary energy body is where the creative power of our mind becomes one with the universal or divine mind of the Creator. It is spiritually perceived as beams of radiant golden and crystalline white light, and it also forms the auric field of protection of which all of our energy bodies are contained. It radiates a protective force of light around us and vibrates at a superfast speed that creates sound similar to a hummingbird.

We are unlimited in our Spirit and in our ability to create our life experiences in the highest and best way. The problem is that we forget this, and we allow our limitations to take root and therefore we interfere with the creative power of our mind and our soul's light. When we create from a place of fear and lack, we move out of harmony with the immense creative power of our causal body of light. When we create from a place of love for the good of all, we expand our causal body, and our whole vibration becomes enlightened in its resonance. We become more open to universal intelligence and to the new ideas yet to be created that could bring benefit to the world in some way.

Our causal body also contains our soul history energies, our karmic energies, our soul's belief patterns, our soul's plan for this lifetime, and our soul's light (quality of consciousness and spiritual wisdom). These all form to create rings of colored light all around our aura, and they influence all aspects of our being. Our causal body also incorporates our innate soul talents garnered from our soul history, and our soul's light contains the spark of our Spirit with all of its unlimited creative power and attributes. We tap into and align with our soul talents and Spirit attributes as we develop our spiritual energies and evolve our consciousness in this lifetime. When we pray, mediate, and gain divine or cosmic inspiration to create something new, we will help expand the light of our causal body. An energy clearing of our causal body can help us align with our spiritual nature, attributes, and soul talents. It can also help us clear energetic interference and imbalances originating from our soul history timeline (past-life and prelife energies) so that we regain more of our soul's creative power. An energy clearing of our auric field can help clear the congestion originating from all of our energy bodies, from the energies absorbed from the environment, and from the energetic exchanges we share with others.

Energy Exchanges

We continuously exchange energies with other people, and at times we are adversely affected by nonbeneficial energy lines, otherwise known as psychic cords. These energy lines can attach anywhere within our aura, within our chakra system, and they even connect directly into the etheric counterpart of our organs, systems, and body parts. In this case, any low vibrational and negative energy that flows through these lines can also interfere with and disturb the integrity and energetic resonance of our organs, systems, and body parts. An energy-clearing treatment of our energy bodies and chakras can help clear and remove any nonbeneficial energy lines of interference. Below is a short description of our body's seven main chakra system.

The Chakra System

ROOT/BASE CHAKRA

The root chakra is located at the base of the spine and is positioned between the anus and the genitals/uterus. Its color resonance is red, and its energy portal connects to our physical body through our adrenal glands. It's energetically aligned with the energy of the planet and helps us ground our energy to Mother Earth. One function of this energy center is to supply us with energy directly emanating from Mother Earth to nourish and vitalize our physical body. If the root chakra shifts off its optimal energetic frequency due to some disturbance or imbalance, then its color, tone, and resonance will alter. This will then limit the optimal flow of energy to the body parts and systems that it governs, and physical dysfunction can set in. In the root chakra's case, it governs over the adrenal glands, skin, genitals, rectum, anus, hips, legs, knees, and feet. Root chakra energy also deals with our ability to feel safe and secure within our environment and with our ability to take care of our body and life's basic needs. Stress over the state of our finances, our property, our job, and our health can cause an energetic imbalance within the root chakra.

SACRAL PLEXUS CHAKRA

The sacral plexus chakra is located in the abdomen, underneath the belly button. Its color resonance is orange, and its energy portal connects to our physical body through our gonads and ovaries/testes. It is energetically aligned with our emotional health and well-being. One function of this energy center is to help us process and integrate our emotions. If the sacral plexus chakra shifts off its optimal energetic frequency due to some disturbance or imbalance, then its color, tone, and resonance will alter. This will then limit the optimal flow of energy to the body parts, organs, and systems that it governs, and physical dysfunction can set in. In the sacral plexus chakra's case, it governs over the abdomen, sexual organs, and reproductive system. Sacral plexus chakra energy also deals with our ability to feel emotionally balanced and creative. Since this energy center deals with our emotional health, blocked creativity and emotional pain cause an energetic imbalance within the sacral plexus chakra.

SOLAR PLEXUS CHAKRA

The solar plexus chakra is located just above the navel. Its color resonance is yellow, and its energy portal connects to our physical body through our pancreas. It is energetically aligned with our mental health and well-being. One function of this energy center is to help us process and integrate our thoughts, beliefs, and opinions and the knowledge we acquire, garnered from our experiences. If the solar plexus chakra shifts off its optimal energetic frequency due to some disturbance or imbalance, then its color, tone, and resonance will alter. This will then limit the optimal flow of energy to the body parts, organs, and systems that it governs, and physical dysfunction can set in. In the solar plexus chakra's case, it governs over the pancreas, digestive system, nervous system, liver, and gallbladder. Solar plexus chakra energy also deals with our ability to feel empowered, confident, and discerning. Since this energy center deals with our mental health, any stress, fear, and nervous tension can cause an energetic imbalance within the solar plexus chakra.

HEART CHAKRA

The heart chakra is located in the center of the chest. Its color resonance is green, and its energy portal connects to our physical body through our thymus gland. It is energetically aligned with our heart and soul energies. One function of this energy center is to help us process the love energy we have. If the heart chakra shifts off its optimal energetic frequency due to some disturbance or imbalance, then its color, tone, and resonance will alter. This will then limit the optimal flow of energy to the body parts, organs, and systems that it governs, and physical dysfunction can set in. In the heart chakra's case, it governs over the thymus gland, immune system, circulatory system, respiratory system, and chest area. Heart chakra energy also deals with our ability to feel unconditional love and compassion for ourselves and others. Since this energy center deals with our heartfelt issues and our relationship connections, any disappointment and deep hurts can cause an energetic imbalance within the heart chakra.

THROAT CHAKRA

The throat chakra is located in the center of our throat. Its color resonance is blue, and its energy portal connects to our physical body through our thyroid gland. It is energetically aligned with our soul's higher truth and creative expression. One function of this energy center is to help us bring our soul's creative expression into being in alignment with the truth and faith. If the throat chakra shifts off its optimal energetic frequency due to some disturbance or imbalance, then its color, tone, and resonance will alter. This will then limit the optimal flow of energy to the body parts, organs, and systems that it governs, and physical dysfunction can set in. In the throat chakra's case, it governs over the thyroid gland, throat, endocrine system, ears, mouth/jaws, and teeth. Throat chakra energy also deals with our ability to express our unique creative talents and to be true to who we are. Since this energy center deals with our creativity and issues of truth and faith, any blocked creative expression and lack of faith in one's abilities can cause an energetic imbalance within the throat chakra.

THIRD-EYE CHAKRA

The third-eye chakra is located in the center of the forehead. Its color resonance is indigo, and its energy portal connects to our physical body through our pituitary gland. It is energetically aligned with our intuitive nature. One function of this energy center is to process our high sense perception. If the third-eye chakra shifts off its optimal energetic frequency due to some disturbance or imbalance, then its color, tone, and resonance will alter. This will then limit the optimal flow of energy to the body parts, organs, and systems that it governs, and physical dysfunction can set in. In the third-eye chakra's case, it governs over the pituitary gland, nervous system, sinuses, eyes, parts of the brain, and head area. Third-eye chakra energy also deals with our ability to visualize our life purpose and to bring this vision into reality. Since this energy center deals with our intuition and our high sense perceptions, any fear of our future and any limiting perceptions about ourselves, others, and the world can cause an energetic imbalance within the third-eye chakra.

Crown Chakra

The crown chakra is located at the top of our head, the crown area. Its color resonance is violet/white, and its energy portal connects to our physical body through our pineal gland. It is energetically aligned with our higher self and God (or the divine mind or universal intelligence or nature). One function of this energy center is to help us process our spiritual nature into physical reality. If the crown chakra shifts off its optimal energetic frequency due to some disturbance or imbalance, then its color, tone, and resonance will alter. This will then limit the optimal flow of energy to the body parts, organs, and systems that it governs, and physical dysfunction can set in. In the crown chakra's case, it governs over the pineal gland, parts of the brain, the skull, the cranium, the bones, and the head area. Crown chakra energy also deals with our ability to feel connected to universal support and the oneness we share with all others. Since this energy center deals with our spiritual nature, any feelings of being separated from God and the universe can cause an energetic imbalance within the crown chakra.

CHAPTER 5

HOUSE ANATOMY

Architecture is really about well-being. I think that people want to feel good in a space. On the one hand it's about shelter, but it's also about pleasure.

—ZAHA HADID

Our home is where our heart is, meaning that it's a sanctuary for our inner being to feel safe, secure, and happy. Taking care of the energy of our home environment will help nurture us so we may feel settled and happy, and these are the best ingredients for health and harmony. The energy of our home environment is a personal extension and reflection of our consciousness. Cluttered areas are also physical representations and manifestations of a cluttered mind. Our choices of furniture, color, objects, and artwork all reflect our personal tastes, and they all input their energetic vibrations directly into the atmosphere of the home environment. Yet, there is also another fascinating aspect of our property that makes up a home, and that is the house anatomy. Just like we have our own physical, energetic, and spiritual anatomy, as explained in the previous chapter, so does a property have its own combined physical, energetic, and spiritual energies that make up the home. Restoring balance and harmony to the house anatomy can also help support our own energetic and spiritual equilibrium. This insightful chapter will reveal all about the different aspects of the house anatomy, how different parts of the home relate to our body and consciousness, and how to help elevate the overall vibration of the home through the choice of color resonance.

The House Anatomy

The house anatomy begins with the architectural design and etheric structure of the home. Next follows all the material and substances that go into creating and building the home to its intended blueprint specifications. Any future changes to the original blueprint pattern of the home, such as adding an extension or knocking down some interior wall, will sometimes disturb the energetic balance of the original etheric structure. The physical wall may be gone, yet its energetic counterpart will still exist. The way that this can cause a disturbance within the home will be through a chaotic energy resonating within and around the empty space and affecting whatever furniture may be placed there. This can cause the space to feel energetically uncomfortable, and it may take some time for someone to feel settled there. However, this disturbance is only temporary as the energetic changes begin to process and fully integrate the new additions or the removed partitions so that a more harmonious energy resonance is restored. It is also easily rectified with a house energy-clearing treatment to help update the original etheric blueprint to its new design. Let's take a look at each aspect of the house anatomy and how it relates to the people who live there.

THE ETHERIC ASPECT OF THE PROPERTY

The etheric aspect of the home underlies the physical structure of the home, since it precedes the foundations and building. It combines all the energies that make up the shell of the property, and includes all of the fabric and substances used to create and build the home: bricks, cement, plaster, wood for the framework, the electrical system, the plumbing system, tiles for the roof, foundations, insulation, air-conditioning, windows, doors, garage, etc. All these things have their own etheric pattern and unique vibration that will emit their energy frequencies into the home. The architectural blueprint pattern and structure of the home will also hold their own unique frequency of their original design. Any changes to this design at a later date will temporarily disturb the etheric layout of the home, which as previously mentioned can be easily rectified. Some people believe they have paranormal activity happen within their home after they've made dramatic interior and exterior changes to the home. This is not necessarily so, because such disturbances can be caused by the building work shifting the etheric balance, since they will be changing the original blueprint pattern created by the architect. Original designs and patterns are points of origin, and any energetic imbalance created through the disturbance of interior or exterior design can be harmonized with the original blueprint. Paranormal activity can be a possibility at times when there are home improvements, simply due to any previous owners' energetic attachment to the property, which can activate when the property's energy is disturbed. This is easily rectified with a house energy-clearing treatment.

Foundation and Structure

The foundation and structure of the home are energetically symbolic of the skeletal, skin, and muscular systems of the human body. Any problems with the foundation, the shell of the house, or the walls, windows, doors, and roof of the home can at times represent temporary energetic challenges to our skin, bones, muscles, and joints, which create our own physical framework. We can make energetic adjustments and repairs to the home that will energetically support us. We are always interacting with the energies of our home environment. Just as the foundations of the home represent grounding and strength to support the overall property, so do they represent how we are able to ground and support our own physical needs. Do we feel safe, secure, and settled in our home environment? Are we able to support ourselves financially? Do we have healthful boundaries that prevent us from being energetically drained? Any problems in the home environment can be a direct reflection of our internal state of consciousness. Why? Because everything external to us, including our home, is the energetic result of our consciousness projecting itself onto reality. We have unlimited creative power within us to change what we don't like the look of, or the experience of so that we can upgrade our personal reality to something more fulfilling. Because everything is energetically connected, we can both adjust and repair issues at a physical level, which can help shift energy, just like a chiropractor does to the spine to help the bones move back into place. We can also adjust things at an energetic level, which again can help shift energy that will correct and support any physical problems.

When doing an energy-clearing treatment on the etheric aspect of the home, we help clear the energetic stagnation and imbalances that are behind any physical dysfunction. We can also make the necessary physical corrections and repairs by taking action. An energy-clearing treatment also works well to help prevent an accumulation of energetic problems from manifesting, because we clear them at the energetic level before they have a chance to reach the physical form.

Betty had painful joints and suffered from arthritis, and so she contacted me for help when her condition worsened. Upon connecting to the energy of her home environment, I found out that the overall vibration there was chaotic due to energetic stress resonating within the home. Betty had decided to remodel her home and was having an extension and a new kitchen fitted. The stress of this project, which cost more and took longer than expected, and the inconvenience of changing her normal daily routine had an adverse effect on her energy levels and her emotional energy body. While she usually manages her arthritis with medication, the excess stress and the chaotic energy of the home made her symptoms more aggravated. The changes in her external environment mirrored the changes going on within her internal environment. She was of course happy about having an additional new room and a new kitchen, yet she was concerned about the transformation, how long it would take, the cost, and the inconvenience. All these energies interplay with what is happening on the physical level in the property. Delays and further problems can set in on the physical level because the energy is imbalanced and chaotic. I energetically cleared both her personal energy fields and the energy of the property so there would be harmony with the building work and with the new additions. Within twenty-four hours she noticed less pain and inflammation, and she felt more inner peace about the new extension and building work.

The Emotional Aspect of the Property

The emotional aspect of the home is connected to the emotions of everyone who's connected to the property, as well as to the feelings that the home generates for us. Its physical representation is the property's plumbing system. We can find great comfort in the sanctuary of our home environment, since we feel nurtured and protected from the elements and from the stress that comes with different life conditions. Whenever we feel sick, we just want to go home, go to bed, and start the healing process. If we don't feel happy or comfortable in our home environment, then not only does this cause a disturbance within our personal energy fields, typically our emotional body, but it can also cause an energetic disturbance within the emotional aspect of the home. The love energy that makes a home feel homely will become depleted, and this can then affect the etheric aspect of the home and its physical counterparts. Water energy is connected to the plumbing system and our emotional body. Any accumulated emotional-energy charges emanating from the family members who live in the home can be reflected in the condition of the property's pluming system, pipes, and water flow. When there are any plumbing problems such as leaks, burst pipes, flooding, toilet problems, or simple water problems such as constantly dripping taps, then this can be an energetic mirror reflecting back to us information about our and other family members' emotional state and well-being.

The Mental Aspect of the Property

The mental aspect of the home is connected to the thoughts of everyone connected to the property and to the thoughts that the home generates for us. Its physical representation is the property's electrical system and wiring. We may think a variety of positive and negative thoughts about our home regarding its condition, design, layout, look, and function. We may have ideas about what we want to do to our home, including making any additional changes to it. We may dream of moving and relocating to a bigger home or downsizing. Our thoughts about the home affect the mental aspect of the property and can either support it, through us expressing beneficial thoughts, or can interfere with it, through us expressing negative thoughts. Our own mental stress, worries, fear, and nervous tension also emit their electrical thought forms directly into the atmosphere of the property and to the mental aspect of the home. This erratic energy can then become reflected in the electrical system of the property. Fuses can blow, electrical problems may persist, and issues with objects that require an electrical input can break down. Toasters, ovens, microwaves, lamps, dishwashers are just some of the things that can go faulty.

The Spiritual Heart/Soul Aspect of the Property

The spiritual heart-and-soul aspect of the property supports the flow of vital energy within, throughout, and around the property and is the heartbeat and unity energy of the home. Its physical representation is reflected in keeping all working parts and functions of the property in good order and harmony. All systems integrate and work harmoniously together and also as separate units. The gas, the electric, the water, the structure and design of the property, and the flow and function of each room of the household. The heart/soul energy aspect provides vital energy and function to the property and is what supports the daily maintenance. Ongoing family arguments, heartbreak, separation, divorce, and trauma can be reflected into the physical aspect of the property as neglected areas of the home or through many things breaking down or causing problems. Often this can happen at the same time or with one issue following the other. Raising the love energy within the home (chapter 8) can help restore the heart/soul energy of the home to support all aspects of the home and all family members in the highest and best way.

The Spiritual Creative Aspect of the Property

The creative-expression aspect of the property involves the energy field of sound, communication, style, and color. It also contains the spiritual template pattern of the property's architectural design. This template pattern sustains the physical manifestation of the property. We can think of it as the hologram of the home. The physical representation of the creative-energy aspect of the property is reflected in the way that the family communicates with each other. Are we able to speak our truth to our family members without fear of us being judged or unsupported? It also involves our use of color, style, and sound within the property: the home's interior design and our inclusion of artwork, feature colors, furniture, fabrics, etc. plus the books that we read; the music we listen to; the emails, posts, and letters we write; the family games we play; and the TV shows and movies we watch.

The Spiritual Celestial Aspect of the Property

The celestial aspect of the property creates an energy field of beautiful shimmering rainbow light that overshadows the property. It generates the necessary spiritual power and vibrational frequency required to connect the guardian or spirit of the home with the actual property. This celestial energy field exudes love energy, and this is what enables a home to keep its spirit guardian, since celestial love is the cosmic ingredient that brings harmony to all. If the property is abused in any way through physical vandalization and destruction of the home or due to it being demolished for whatever reason, then the celestial energy field of the property will draw back its radiant light to the celestial realm. Lack of love, respect, and appreciation of the property also disconnects the celestial light energy from overshadowing the property. This disconnect interferes with connecting the guardian of the home to the property. This means that the guardian or spirit of the home is no longer required to watch over the property, and they also return their energy back to their relevant dimension of light. Black magic, curses, black masses, violence, and abuse within the property also diminish the celestial light and protective spiritual power of the guardian of the property, which makes the property become more vulnerable to spiritual infestation.

The Spiritual–Guardian Aspect of the Property

The spiritual-guardian aspect of the property is a benevolent light being that oversees the care of the overall property and its inhabitants. The spiritual guardian makes sure that the property stays intact, and disconnects its light, as previously mentioned, only if the property is being demolished or if it is being misused in some way. When there is a breakdown in alignment with the spiritual guardian of the property, the protective aura of the home can be compromised. A harmonious home filled with love and joy energy will greatly nurture the care and attention of the spiritual guardian. Prayer for spiritual and physical protection for the home will invoke the spiritual cocreative power for the guardian of the home to be actively assisting. Offering gratitude to God, the universe, the angels, or whoever aligns with your belief system for helping to protect your property is an important spiritual step. Gratitude mixed with faith in benevolent spiritual assistance is what will create powerful results.

Natural disasters and forest fires can destroy and damage many homes, and although this is an environmental cause of destruction and something that is outside our control, we can still invoke the spiritual guardian of our property to help take care of our property and land in the highest and best way. In this sense, even though damage may be inevitable due to the location of the property and the circumstances at hand, there may be less damage done than there could have been, and also unexpected assistance to help rebuild. There have been many stories where people have prayed over their homes for protection in the face of approaching destruction, and their homes and their heartfelt personal items have remained intact.

What about the harmful personal intentions of others toward our property? The spiritual guardian of the property generates an energy force field of light that helps deflect all harmful intentions, such as those looking to break into the property. Since this is a cocreative process, we must also do what we can on a physical level to help protect our property from such low consciousness interference by taking protective measures. Both physical and spiritual intervention works in harmony as a preventive measure.

I was contacted by a lady in Ireland who was scared about her home being broken into by a gang of thugs. Her son had gotten mixed up with drugs, and it was known that he owed some money to drug dealers and they wanted their payment. The son had left home a few years before, and only the lady and her young daughter remained in the family home. The lady mentioned that for the previous two nights a carful of men sat near the gate at the end of their home, just watching and waiting for any sign of the lady's son. She felt scared and intimidated for her and for her daughter, and yet she didn't want to call the police since she knew there would be repercussions toward her home. This lady asked me for help with a specific prayer for protection for them and their property. I gave her the following prayer visualization, and she began immediately. Within twenty-four hours there were no further visits from this drug gang.

I asked the lady to use her imagination to visualize the following: "Imagine a force field of vibrant white or golden light in the shape of a triangle and see your property sitting within it."

Archangel Michael's divine light frequency works in harmony with the spiritual guardian of the home to place an aura of protective light within and around the property. I would like to tell you that her years of prayers for her son to quit drugs, heal, and make a good life for himself have worked, yet so far it hasn't. This is because prayer works in harmony with the free will of a person. Her son at this present time is not ready to break free from his habit and lifestyle. Seeds of light have been planted in his consciousness through prayer power for whenever he's truly ready, and then help will surely be administered.

PRAYER OF SPIRITUAL PROTECTION

"I ask the light of Archangel Michael to clear my house, property, and land up to an 8-mile radius of all forms of harmful intent and negative energy. I ask for divine light protection within and around [place full names here] and my home so that we are taken care of in the highest and best way. Thank you. Amen. It is done!"

Color Resonance within the Home Environment

When we add color to specific areas of the home environment, we immediately help shift the vibrational frequency in that particular area. Light is the true source of color, and so different color vibrations resonating within the home environment will emit their light energy into the light bodies of our auric fields. This can help elevate our moods through influencing our emotional body and can also help inspire us by influencing our mental and spiritual bodies. The seven colors of our seven main chakras correspond to the seven colors of the rainbow. Color vibrations emanating within the home environment can also help energetically nurture the rainbow colors of our chakra system, which in turn is what energetically supports the vitality and vibration of our organs, systems, and body parts. Different areas of the home are also more suited toward certain colors due to their interaction with our personal energy fields. Too much yellow within the bedroom, for instance, can overstimulate the nervous system, and we may find it more difficult to relax our mind prior to sleep. Indigo blues, violets, and soft greens have a more calming effect on our nervous system and heart energy, and they are more suitable for our sleeping quarters. These colors can help us relax our mind, body, and soul, since our sleep time is the optimal time for regeneration and healing. It is important to choose your own color theme for your home and to trust your inner guidance system, because these will be the colors that your energy body will seeking. The following colors reveal what their specific light frequencies can add to our home environment and their influence on our personal energies. Trust your instincts and go with what is best and right for you.

Red Tones: Action, Success, Passion, Chemistry

The color red is energizing, activating, vitalizing, and powerful. It is a wonderful color to utilize within the home environment, since it emanates a warm and invigorating feeling to our senses. A red front door gives character and charm to the home, and both red and green energy symbolize the frequency of abundance. Including both of these colors within the home environment can help us attract and create greater levels of abundance energy within our lives, purely due to the vibrational resonance being offered to us. The way that this works is that red energy (action, passion, and success) as well as green energy (abundance, giving, receiving, unconditional love, and harmony) merge with our aura energy to create a magnetic field of light within and around us that then directs and pulls to us life experiences and opportunities that will generate greater abundance within our lives. Red energy also aligns with our root chakra and supports life energy, which influences the vital health and strength of our physical body and how well we manage our life experience. If we lack energy and drive, by including some red energy within the home it can help vitalize and motivate us. Too much red energy within the home can elevate any aggressive tendencies we have within us, since it has a direct influence on our adrenal glands and blood pressure. Using red as a feature wall within our living space or dining room is a grand choice, and one that can help us physically connect and respond to each other. A little red energy in the bedroom is also fine and will help boost our romance energies and our passion and chemistry, yet too much red energy within the bedroom can be too energizing and keep us awake. Red energy within the office area can help us generate the energy and passion it requires to get a project going.

ORANGE TONES: CREATIVITY, FEELINGS, JOY, MOVEMENT

The color orange is creative, joyful, and vitalizing. It is a wonderful color to utilize within the home environment, since it exudes vitality and sparks joy. An orange front door expresses the owner's joy of entertaining and of their social connection with others. Including orange energy within the home environment can help us attract and create greater levels of creativity, friendship, and joy within our lives due to the vibrational resonance being offered to us. Orange energy also aligns with our sacral plexus chakra and supports the energy of new beginnings and excitement, which influences the movement of our ideas into the reality of our life experience. Too much orange energy within the home can trigger our emotional energies since it has a direct influence on our emotional body. If you are depressed, then adding some orange energy to the home is an excellent way to help uplift you and get your creative energy moving again. Using orange as a feature wall within our kitchen or dining room is a creative choice and one that can help us enjoy our activities there. It can also help us connect with each other on an emotional level, so we get to enjoy our social connection with each other. A little orange in the bedroom is also fine and will help with the fertility process due to the creative power of orange energy on our reproductive systems. Orange energy within the office area can help excite us with new ideas and the enthusiasm required to begin new projects.

YELLOW TONES: INTELLECT, CONFIDENCE, WILLPOWER, MOTIVATION

The color yellow is logical, positive, and motivating. It is a wonderful color to utilize within the home environment since it emanates positive energy and sparks confidence. A yellow front door expresses the owner's positive, sunny nature and attitude. Including yellow energy within the home environment can help us tap into our positive, happy side and inspire us mentally to be confident and decisive about our personal choices, due to the vibrational resonance being offered to us. Yellow energy also aligns with our solar plexus chakra and supports our digestive health, metabolism, and mental well-being. Too much yellow energy within the home can elevate any hyperactive tendencies within us, since it has a direct influence on our mindset. If you lack confidence, then adding yellow energy to the home is an excellent way to help empower and motivate you into taking positive action. Using yellow as a feature wall within our kitchen or dining room can help light up the area with happy vibes and help us intellectually connect with each other. Yellow energy within the office area can help us intellectually communicate with others and support us in making clear decisions about our business goals.

Green Tones: Harmony, Abundance, Giving/ Receiving, Unconditional Love

The color green is harmonious, balanced, and abundant. It is a wonderful color to utilize within the home environment, since it emanates harmony and unconditional love. A green front door expresses the owner's heart-centered nature and their ability to connect with others at a heart and soul level. Including green energy within the home environment can help us attract and create greater levels of abundance (as aforementioned in the red energy), plus establish heart/soul relationships in our lives. Green energy also aligns with our heart chakra and supports our compassionate nature, which influences our engagement with others and the world in which we live. Too much green energy within the home can make us overly concerned with other people's needs, and we can begin to neglect our own. It's all about creating balance in our home, in our personal energy fields, and in our life. If you are heartbroken, then adding green energy to the home is an excellent way to help heal the hurt you've experienced at a heart/soul level. Using green as a feature wall within our kitchen or dining room can help us feel comfort in our home's environment, as well as bringing comfort to our family unit. Green energy in the bedroom will help relax the body and mind and can aid in the regeneration of our body's energy as we sleep, since green and blue energies are great healing forces. Green energy also helps harmonize our body's immune system. Green energy in the office area can help us utilize our compassionate nature in service of others and can support the energy of abundance and prosperity within our business opportunities.

Blue Tones: Strength, Healing, Truth, Protection

The color blue is strong, expressive, and healing. It is a wonderful color to utilize within the home environment, since it emanates inner strength and sparks communication. A blue front door expresses the owner's integrity and their value of truth and ability to easily express themselves to others. Including blue energy within the home environment can help us express our opinions to others in an appropriate manner and have the courage to communicate the truth of our inner being within our life experience. Blue energy also aligns with our throat chakra and supports all aspects of communication, including listening to others, speaking, singing, writing, drawing, dancing, and any other forms of creative expression. Too much blue energy within the home can make us become very authoritative and bossy. If you are suffering from chronic illness and have persisting aches and pains, then adding blue energy to the home is an excellent way to help support the body's wisdom to heal itself. Using blue as a feature wall within our kitchen or dining room can help us enjoy our communication with others and express our inner being. Blue energy in the bedroom is wonderful to help with promoting inner peace and relaxation. Blue energy also helps balance our endocrine system and hormonal balance. Blue energy in the office area can help us connect and communicate more clearly with our customers, staff, and clients, and it can help us tap into greater levels of creativity within our specialized niche.

Indigo Tones: Intuition, Manifestation, Imagination, Relaxation

The color indigo is intuitive, peaceful, and imaginative. It is a wonderful color to utilize within the home environment, since it emanates inner peace and sparks the imagination. An indigo front door expresses the owner's ability to dream big and think outside the box. Including indigo energy within the home environment can help us perceive our obstacles from a higher-elevated perspective that can help us shift our limited thinking. Indigo energy also aligns with our third-eye chakra and supports our intuitive nature and our imagination. Too much indigo energy within the home can cause us to become too dreamy about our life's goals without us taking any necessary action. If you are suffering with headaches, then adding indigo energy to the home is an excellent way to help ease your nervous tension. Using indigo as a feature wall within our kitchen or dining room can help us intuitively connect with each other and express our dreams and desires. Indigo energy in the bedroom can help us meditate and sleep and is especially good for those who suffer from insomnia. Indigo energy calms our nervous system. Indigo energy in the office area can help us utilize our intuitive nature in service of others and within our business opportunities.

Violet Tones: Wisdom, Transformation, Connection, Destiny

The color violet is transformative, freeing, and guiding. It is a wonderful color to utilize within the home environment, since it emanates wisdom and sparks our inner purpose. A violet front door expresses the owner's joy of connecting with others at a spiritual level. Including violet energy within the home environment can help us align with our destiny and life purpose, as well as help us be open for transformation. Violet energy also aligns with our crown chakra and supports our spiritual energies and our universal connection with all. Too much violet energy within the home can elevate feelings of self-importance and elitism. If you are overly left brained and rational minded, then adding violet energy to the home is an excellent way to help you to connect with your spiritual side and receive higher guidance. Using violet as a feature wall within our kitchen or dining room can help us spiritually connect with others and express our innate wisdom when required. Violet energy in the bedroom will help calm our spirit and nervous tension. Violet energy in the office area can help us connect with our inner guidance system and universal intelligence as we move forward along our life purpose and destiny.

White: Purification, Protection, Peace

The color white is purifying, protecting, and peaceful. It is a wonderful color to utilize within the home environment, since it emanates purification and sparks peacefulness. A white front door expresses the owner's sense of style—one that is organized, simplistic, and clean. Including white energy within the home environment can help us create feelings of inner peace and beauty, as well as making the rooms feel more spacious. White energy also aligns with our crown chakra just as the violet energy does, and it supports our spiritual connection with our soul's higher self. Too much white energy within the home can elevate feelings of isolation. If you are fearful, then adding white energy to the home is an excellent way to help you to feel spiritually protected. Using white as a feature wall within our kitchen or dining room can help convey freshness and cleanliness, and it can generate feelings of peace in our connection with each other. White energy in the bedroom will help with clearing our mind and calming our emotions prior to sleep. White energy in the office area can help us utilize our peaceful nature as a way to restore harmony to any challenging circumstances.

Black: Mystery, Power, Grounding

The color black is mysterious, powerful, and grounding. It is a wonderful color to utilize within the home environment, since it emanates grounding and order. A black front door expresses the owner's joy, classic style, and mysterious nature. Including black energy within the home environment can help ground our chaotic energies and generate a feeling of calm. Too much black energy within the home can trigger limiting and negative thoughts and fears. If you feel vulnerable and lack confidence, then adding black energy to the home is an excellent way to help empower you. Using black as a feature wall within our living room or dining room not only adds a classic style to the room can also help us tap into our mysterious nature and enjoy this aspect of ourselves in our social connection with each other. A little black energy in the bedroom is also fine and will help us switch off from the stress of the day or from any current challenges we may be going through. Black energy in the office area can help us feel decisive and powerful in our decision-making and grounded in times of personal stress.

PART 2

PLUGGING IN—CREATIVE CLEARING POWER

CHAPTER 6

SPIRITUAL ASSISTANCE

For he shall give his angels charge over thee to keep thee in all thy ways.
—Psalm 91:11 (KJV)

"Angels, I need help fast" was my first prayer of the night uttered out loud as I reversed my car into a snow-covered ditch after turning to go down the wrong secluded country lane. With everything covered in snow and still snowing, I was slightly disoriented. The car was firmly stuck, and I was alone with no phone signal. It was about 7:30 p.m. and completely dark as I was heading home from my local town after a day of shopping with friends and dinner. I lived with my husband in a house located very high up on top of a mountain near the world-famous Loch Ness, in Scotland. After several minutes staying stuck in the ditch and processing the situation, I quickly surrendered to the fact that there was nothing that I could physically do myself to fix this situation, plus I couldn't contact my husband since my cell phone had no signal, and he had no idea I was on my way home, so once more I asked for spiritual help. For my second prayer of the night, I actually placed my hands in the prayer position. I've been praying like this for so long that my brain waves relax, and my subconscious mind is immediately activated by this tangible physical action. While of course there is no need to hold your hands together in the prayer position to engage in the act of prayer, I find by doing so it is a simple act of faith that sets things in motion. By expressing even just a little amount of faith will generate more than enough spiritual energy to cocreate miracles—or in my case, to intervene and help me in my hour of need. My second prayer was more specific, and I asked the angels to please let my husband know that I needed help and to come and find me. It was about a fifteen-minute drive to my house from where I was stuck, and I was too scared to walk the dark, isolated country road home by myself, and so I just sat and waited. In my heart, I knew I would be okay, and that help would arrive. While I never heard a spiritual voice or saw any angels appearing, about twenty minutes later I suddenly heard a car pull up, and a young man approached my car window. He had spotted my headlights and came to check if I was okay. I was so thankful of being found and thought the angels must have done the next best thing by sending this man my way. However, another car also began to approach, and as it got nearer, I could see that it was my husband. He said that all of a sudden, he had gotten an intuitive feeling that something was wrong and that he should go and look for me. This feeling was the result of the angels impressing their message upon his consciousness, which then alerts his intuitive nature. This is one of the most common ways that spiritual help is delivered to us when we are open to receive it. In other cases of spiritual intervention, angels have been known to appear and then disappear once the help has been administered. We thanked the young man, left my car in the ditch until daylight, and headed off home. My husband told me that he was working on the computer and suddenly he felt the energy shift around him. He then received an inner knowing that he needed to come find me. He said it was like receiving information without any words being spoken, yet it was accompanied with a strong compulsion to go find me. I've never forgotten this day because of the spiritual help I received through the power of prayer and angelic intervention.

The Power of Prayer

To pray is to be active in cocreation with the benevolent forces of the universe rather than doing nothing or attempting to do something in our own limited power. Prayer power is activated from the inside out, since it is instigated by our heart and soul energy plus our mental focus, which then combines together to generate and release extraordinary spiritual power. Prayer is what links you to the benevolent forces of the universe and enables you to tap into a greater creative power source of which you are eternally connected. When our soul's light links up to the universal field of Light, then we will naturally amplify the creative power within us through the act of cocreation. This is what Catherine Ponder has to say about what happens when we pray:

> When you pray, you stir into action an atomic force. You release a potent spiritual vibration that can be released in no other way. Through prayer you unleash a God energy within and around you that gets busy working for you and through you, producing right attitudes, reactions, and results. It is your prayers that recognize and release that God power.

The power of prayer will align you with greater creative power to help you make atomic transformational changes within an environment or within a person's bio-auric fields and etheric energy body. There are benevolent forces and beings of cosmic Light that are always ready and willing to join cocreative forces with you for the good of all. It is through prayer power that our consciousness can connect with enlightened spiritual assistance. This kind of spiritual assistance will help prevent you from experiencing energetic interference as you do your energy-clearing work. Prayer power offers you access to spiritual protection and provides you with the necessary spiritual support as you perform your energy-clearing treatments. Within this chapter you will discover how to develop greater prayer power by using a specific creative technique that will have you glowing with light energy. You will also be shown how to safely and intuitively align and cocreate with benevolent spiritual assistance through the expansion of your heart and soul energy and through the concentrated focus of your mind. All three energetic forces of the heart, soul, and mind will merge together and generate one superpowerful spiritual frequency. Expanding your cosmic consciousness in this way enables you to plug in to the higher dimensions of Light frequencies to utilize them for extraordinary, transformational energy-clearing work.

Faith and Trust

Prayer has always been a significant part of my daily life experience from a very early age, after being taught to pray in kindergarten. Because of this, I've established deep faith and trust in its innate spiritual power. Faith and trust are also the necessary spiritual ingredients that help give our prayers wings of light to generate the creative power we require for intervention to take place. We are not required to have a certain amount of unwavering faith in order to set things in motion, since having just a seed of faith is more than enough spiritual energy required to invite universal support our way. The same can be said for our ability to trust that our prayers have been received and answered. Having even a small amount of trust will help create the energetic resonance required within our personal auric fields to help us attract and create whatever it is we are praying for—whether this be a prayer request for us or for someone else. Missing out on these two spiritual ingredients can interfere with and delay our prayer power results.

PRAYER CHANGES THINGS

In my healing office I have a small wooden sign that reads "Prayer Changes Things." Prayer is my light switch to tap into the creative power of the universe and to align with the benevolent universal forces of Light. Prayer is my go-to response for so many things in my life, from needing spiritual guidance on any given topic, to asking for spiritual protection, to expressing gratitude, to petitioning help for others, to manifesting personal desires, to empowering my energy-clearing work. Prayer enables me to connect with and direct the cosmic healing forces of Creation through my clear intent and my expanded heart energy.

Prayer is not some mysterious supernatural force that works only for those who are religious, attend church, or are spiritually minded. Anyone can pray if they set their heart/mind energy to it, because everyone has a soul, and the energy of the human soul is always intimately connected to the energy of the universe.

How Prayer Works

When you pray from your heart and soul energy, meaning that you are heart centered in your prayer request, it will instigate your spiritual alignment with universal energy, and you will naturally expand your consciousness. Praying from a place of fear energy, needy energy, and greedy energy all involves low vibrational frequencies that are out of harmony with universal love, and with our authentic spiritual nature. This means that they fail to generate enough heart/soul energy to instigate a clear and strong spiritual alignment with universal support to cocreate our prayer requests. We can then falsely believe that some source outside us, typically God, is against our prayers being answered. The truth is that universal support is always there and is always ready and waiting for us to cocreate together, and the secret of this is truly simple: it is love energy that greatly empowers our spiritual alignment and unlimited support. God energy is the energy of our Spirit, the spark of creative consciousness and Light that enables our soul to have a human experience. As previously mentioned, God energy is within us, yet it also exists as a magnificent external universal force of Love energy of which we are all interconnected. There is no separation between us. Love energy unites us, and fear energy creates the illusion of separation.

Once we have expanded our heart and soul energy for cosmic alignment, prayer power works through the clear mental focus of a concentrated mind. Our prayer request, petition, or directive (prayer command) then sets in motion cosmic frequencies of light that contain celestial intelligence and the specific energy required to instigate transformational shifts. This process is what provides the necessary spiritual power required to make alchemical changes within the physical realm and within atomic matter. Alchemical shifts will begin to transform, clear, release, or correct any nonbeneficial energies, interference, and dysfunction. This is what the late, world-renowned spiritual healer Harry Edwards said about distance-healing prayer.

Absent healing is prayer plus directive intercession through the attunement with God's healing ministers in spirit, who administer the healing directive. Absent healing is a spirit science involving a more advanced and special technique. It only needs a little consideration to see that when a patient is healed from a severe or incurable malady without any physical contact with a healer, we have evidence of a far more evolved science. To appreciate the modus operandi of absent healing, it is obvious that it arises from thought processes, as far as the healer is concerned. This must be so for the healing originates from the mental request for healing to reach the patient, and thus this is the primary factor which sets healing in motion.

These words come from one of the most remarkable spiritual healers of the last one hundred years. Thousands of people from all walks of life, from all nationalities and religions, have been helped through the intercessory prayers of Harry Edwards, and many of these people were suffering from diseases said by doctors to be "incurable." What this tells us is that Harry Edwards intimately understood the power of prayer, the power of mental activity, and the power of an expanded heart as he linked into the universal realm of creative power to help make alchemical changes within the world of matter. When you understand about your own ability to utilize prayer power through applying the energies already within you, then you will have access to miraculous creative potential. Miracles arise from higher spiritual laws that are not yet fully understood by our level of consciousness. While there are natural laws of nature that pertain to the physical realm, there are also higher creative laws of spiritual power that are beyond our understanding. It is these higher vibrational laws of spiritual power that can supersede the laws of nature within the physical realm to make significant transformation when the conditions are harmonious.

Human Interference with Prayer Power

Some people contest that their prayers don't get answered and that therefore praying is fake, false, and not worth their effort. Yet, for others, they say that their prayers were definitely heard and answered. Why does one person's prayer get answered, and another person's prayer fail? The truth is that there are many reasons for this, and here are four reasons for why some prayers aren't answered and don't work. Yet, all four reasons can be transcended.

Reason 1: Wanting God to do something for you without understanding your own part in the creation of your life's story.

This suggests that you are separate from God and universal energy, since you perceive God as a force outside yourself and one that grants wishes and desires on the basis of merit and karma. By understanding our eternal connection to unlimited universal support that is always available for us, 24/7, and that all we need to do to cocreate with this cosmic support is to be in greater harmony with love energy in our thoughts, words, beliefs, and actions as best we can, then we can consciously create a fulfilling life. Yes, we may have many stressful days, weeks, and months because we are upset, annoyed, angry, hurt, and frustrated. Life challenges and obstacles come and go, yet all we need to do is to remember that we are extraordinary creative beings with universal support. By remembering the truth of our soul, we begin to tap into our creative potential, and we will draw back our soul power in order to help transform our life stressors instead of reacting to them. Karmic interference is also cleared through the soul's expression and service of love energy. No obstacle in our life is therefore permanent.

Reason 2: Lack of mental focus

Some people pray without giving any creative effort to their prayer. They may be repeating words to the universe, while at the same time they are also thinking about what they are having for dinner later that evening or thinking of something else. A clear mental focus generates greater creative power of the mind so that prayer requests, petitions, and commands are set in motion. Once you have received feedback of helping another through utilizing the creative power of your mental energy, you will be encouraged to keep strengthening your mental focus.

Reason 3: Feeling unworthy of your prayer being heard and answered

Lack of self-love and self-worth interferes with prayer power because you judge yourself harshly. Self-criticism and harsh judgments create the illusionary separation from universal support due to being out of harmony with universal love. Self-love and a healthy amount of self-worth align with your authentic spiritual nature and are in harmony with universal support.

Reason 4: Unwilling to forgive others

Unforgiveness generates a spiritual resistance in the heart and soul energy and within the auric fields that can interfere with the expansion of consciousness. Yet, it's not necessary to forgive someone if you "can" let go of the hurt, anger, and all the negative thoughts that connect to the experience. The letting-go process is often enough to help clear the resistance energy. However, forgiveness is a spiritual trait and one that often follows later after the letting-go process. The act of letting go frees the heart energy, and then the soul becomes more expressive with the love of its authentic spiritual nature.

How to Pray Powerful Prayers

Without the spiritual formula of our expanded heart and soul energy combined with a clear mind and greatly encouraged by the spiritual ingredients of faith and trust, our prayer petitions may remain vibrationally bound within the atmosphere of the earth realm. This is because they lack the creative power to gain enough spiritual momentum to elevate into the realms of Light. Supernatural prayer power is the result of the spiritual formula that skyrockets the prayer petition into the higher dimensions of creative light and the universal forces of Love. Prayer power and prayer results are also intimately associated with our specific level and quality of consciousness, frequency, and vibration. The way that this works is because of our Spirit's relationship with Absolute Love. This perfect force of Absolute Love has no judgment, no punishment, no error in consciousness, and no yin/yang or dual nature and polarity. The cosmic seed of Absolute Love exists as a beacon of Light within our Spirit and is what illuminates our heart and soul energy with attributes of this perfect love and universal intelligence. Whenever we expand our heart and soul energy via nonjudgment, neutrality, harmony, unconditional love, and creative service, then we release more light within us, and we amplify its glow. The amount of light, love, and wisdom emerging from within us is what generates the strength of our creative power. Since more light equals more creative power, then it stands to reason that we will have greater access to cocreate with the higher dimensional realms of universal support. Our consciousness will continue to evolve in this way as we bring more of our authentic spiritual nature into our physical reality. The quality of our consciousness therefore also super-amplifies our prayer results. The following healing-prayer-treatment exercise will help you clear your energy, elevate your vibration, and expand your consciousness to help take your prayer power to the next level. It is also an excellent healing treatment to support the body's vital health and well-being.

ALIGNMENT WITH LOVE PRAYER TREATMENT

Read through the entire exercise first so that you familiarize yourself with it. You can also record the exercise in your own voice and then play it back. Doing this exercise daily will help you memorize it so that it becomes easier each time that you practice. It is a wonderful exercise to include as part of your spiritual routine. Make sure you won't be disturbed as you begin this spiritual exercise, to help you align with the universal energy of absolute love and of your true spiritual nature. When you are ready, take a few slow, deep breaths, in through the nose and out of the mouth, to help calm your nervous system. Relax your body as best you can by sitting comfortably, whether this be sitting up in your bed or in a chair. Let's begin!

I am one with absolute love. I am one with the universe. I am one with the Light. I exist within the body and consciousness of absolute love, and absolute love exists within me. Absolute love resonates within my atoms, molecules, particles, RNA, DNA, cells, organs, systems, and body parts. Absolute love resonates within my mind, body, Spirit, soul, aura, and consciousness. Absolute love resonates within my thoughts, words, beliefs, emotions, attitude, behavior, and actions. I easily express absolute love within my relationships with others. I easily express absolute love within nature. Absolute love and I are one!

INTUITIVE NATURE

You are already intuitive because it's a significant part of your spiritual makeup. Some people rely on their intuitive nature within their jobs, such as detectives, who often have gut instincts. As a result of acknowledging our intuitive faculties, we help naturally fine-tune them. Intuitive vibes begin energetically and can at times be felt in our physical body. We may have reactions such as goose bumps on our skin if we encounter an energy that is different from our own energetic signature. We can take on the physical symptoms of others temporarily when we connect with them. One student of mine was doing an energy-clearing treatment for her friend, and she suddenly felt a sharp pain in her tooth that lasted seconds. She mentioned this to her friend later and found out that the friend had been to the dentist that day due to having a toothache. We also have spiritual senses that help us intuitively and spiritually see, hear, sense, and know information on a subtle energetic and spiritual level. These senses are more often known as clairvoyant (seeing), clairaudient (hearing), clairsentient (sensing/feeling), and claircognizant (knowing). We all have these abilities, and they can be energetically cleared and aligned with love energy in order to help us gain more clarity and understanding when we do our energy-clearing work, and to help us when we connect with benevolent spiritual helpers and universal support. The following intuitive clearing prayer can help you empower your wonderful and remarkable intuitive nature.

Intuitive Clearing Prayer

I ask the Light of Absolute Love to clear my intuitive channels of irrational fear energy, nervous tension, and emotional imbalance. Clear and remove any nonbeneficial energies that interfere with my intuitive alignment to Absolute Love. Restore my ability to clearly discern my intuitive vibes free of all chaotic energies. Thank you, Amen. It is done!

SPIRITUAL COCREATIVE ASSISTANCE

Now that you've aligned with absolute love energy and have cleared and rebalanced your intuitive faculties, it's time to get acquainted with universal support and your unlimited benevolent team of helpers.

The Divine-Light-Clearing Team

You have your very own divine-light-clearing team of benevolent spiritual beings and cosmic forces ready to assist you with cocreative power. Who are these benevolent helpers? First off, they are universal in their support and work with you in the way that you are most comfortable with. If you are religious, then you can call in the support of the Holy Spirit, the Christ Light Consciousness, Mother Mary, and the Angels, et al. However, all of these divine light forces are universal and available to all religious or not. If you feel you would prefer to work with universal forces without any personality associated with them, then you can work with the seven benevolent forces of peace, love, wisdom, strength, healing, transformation, and service. These seven forces are evolved states of consciousness and divine light creative power. They are associated with seven powerful archangels, yet they stand for universal creative powers, which carry extraordinary rays of divine light. It is these forces and streams of universal intelligence that will aid you in your energy-clearing work. You can also decide on whom else you wish to include in your own divine-light-clearing team by who you have a special affinity with, including any spirit guides, guardian angels, spirit loved ones, and ancestors.

How Your Divine-Light-Clearing Team Can Help You

Your divine-light-clearing team cocreates your energy-clearing treatments with you via your specific energy-clearing prayer commands, which you will discover from chapter 8 onward. Through your creative prayer power combined with their cosmic creative power, you both help make the necessary spiritual and energetic adjustments required in your energy-clearing treatments. Once you decide on whom you would like to include in your universal support system, you can group them into what I call a divine-light-clearing team of helpers. To help you become familiar with your divine-light-clearing team, just begin to include them in your thoughts and prayers by sending gratitude to them for assisting you in your energy-clearing work. By including universal support to help you with your energy-clearing treatments, you will form a team of specialized creative assistance for all of your energy-clearing needs. Universal support will also spiritually protect you from energetic and spiritual interference. The following seven cosmic forces of celestial divine light contain specific streams of intelligence, healing power, support, and harmony. Each one also aligns with a celestial archangel. Whether you choose to incorporate them in with your divine-light-clearing team is of personal choice. They are the divine light frequencies that I work with in my energy-clearing treatments, along with my guardian angel, spirit guide, and spirit loved ones. We always connect to universal support and cosmic assistance through our heart and soul energy, which is what provides us with the optimal vibrational access to tap into our higher-self nature.

Seven Cosmic Forces of Divine Light

The Royal-Blue Celestial Stream of Divine Light: Assists us with spiritual protection, the clearing of spiritual interference and attachments, and the provision of spiritual strength.

The royal-blue divine light frequency is aligned with Archangel Michael, whose name means "He who is like God."

The royal-blue stream of divine light emanates directly from the cosmic sun of Absolute Love. This powerful cosmic frequency can break through discordant energy patterns resonating within the home/work environment and within our personal energy fields. Archangel Michael or the royal-blue divine light stream (or both) is the most important angel and frequency to work with for any kind of spiritual infestation, spiritual/psychic attack, and clearing of attachments. Archangel Michael and the royal-blue light can help us overcome our shadow nature and break through limitations that keep us from being our authentic self.

The Golden-Yellow Celestial Stream of Divine Light: Assists us with intuitive knowledge and wisdom and helps restore creative beauty back to any energetic atmosphere, environment, and consciousness.

The golden-yellow divine light frequency is aligned with Archangel Jophiel, whose name means "Beauty of God."

The golden-yellow stream of divine light emanates directly from the cosmic sun of Absolute Love. This enlightened cosmic frequency can help transform any nonbeneficial energies that are out of alignment with their true nature, thus restoring the innate beauty of their creation. Archangel Jophiel or the golden-yellow divine light stream (or both) help uplift the energy within our environments and our own consciousness by beautifying our thoughts, perceptions, and behaviors so that they are in harmony with our authentic nature. In doing so, we become more enlightened, and our intuitive and spiritual alignment to universal support is purified and strengthened.

The Rose-Pink Celestial Stream of Divine Light: Assists us with raising the level of love energy within an environment and within the energetic anatomy of a person and animal. Works to restore harmony and balance back to the atmosphere of the home/work environment and to our personal energies.

The rose-pink divine light frequency is aligned with Archangel Chamuel, whose name means "He who sees/seeks God."

The rose-pink stream of divine light emanates directly from the cosmic sun of Absolute Love. This unconditionally loving cosmic frequency is one of the most powerful healing frequencies for helping restore harmony and joy back to an environment, person, animal, and situation. Archangel Chamuel or the rose-pink divine light frequency (or both) can help clear trauma energies resonating within a home/work environment and within our heart/soul energy. Archangel Chamuel and the rose-pink light can help us expand our heart energy so that we are able to love one another unconditionally, including self-love and acceptance.

The Emerald-Green Celestial Stream of Divine Light: Assists us with energy clearing and healing corrections, restoring balance, and expanding our heart and soul energy to be vibrationally open to receive unlimited abundance.

The emerald-green divine light frequency is aligned with Archangel Raphael, whose names means "God Heals."

The emerald-green stream of divine light emanates directly from the cosmic sun of Absolute Love. This extraordinary cosmic clearing and healing frequency is the ultimate force of healing light. Archangel Raphael or the emerald-green divine light frequency (or both) can help make any necessary energetic corrections within any dysfunctional etheric energy patterns to restore harmony and balance. Archangel Raphael and the emerald-green light can help us expand our heart and soul energy to be more vibrationally aligned with the unlimited support and abundance of the universe. Archangel Raphael and the emerald-green light can help us heal any physical health issues from a spiritual and energetic perspective, so that our physical body harmonizes with optimal energetic flow and function.

The Pure-White Celestial Stream of Divine Light: Assists us with inner strength, insight, and the energetic purification of a person, animal, place, and object.

The pure-white divine light frequency is aligned with Archangel Gabriel, whose name means "God is my strength."

The pure-white stream of divine light emanates directly from the cosmic sun of Absolute Love. This remarkable cosmic frequency is purifying and protective. Archangel Gabriel or the pure-white divine light frequency (or both) can help restore the spirit of inner strength when there is any weakness or dysfunction by clearing and purifying any nonbeneficial energies. Archangel Gabriel and the pure-white light can help us develop inner strength in order to overcome any physical life challenges. Archangel Gabriel and the pure-white light can help clear the adverse energetic effects of any toxic energies within an environment such as geopathic stress. The pure-white light is super-beneficial in helping us empower and ground our polarity connection to Mother Earth. Archangel Gabriel can help in the healing process of all children, especially babies, and can assist in helping couples experiencing fertility issues.

The Purple-Gold with Ruby-Red Celestial Stream of Divine Light: Assists us with restoring the energies of inner peace, love, and harmony.

The purple-gold with ruby-red divine light frequency is aligned with Archangel Uriel, whose name means "Fire/Light of God."

The purple-gold with ruby-red stream of divine light emanates directly from the cosmic sun of Absolute Love. This peaceful cosmic frequency clears fear energy attached to or within a person, animal, place, or object and restores the light of inner peace. Archangel Uriel or the purple-gold with ruby-red light (or both) works to clear the root cause of disharmony within consciousness so that we feel spiritually supported and aligned with love. Archangel Uriel can help inspire and assist us to be of greater service to the world and to others in our soul's unique creative expression of light.

The Violet Celestial Stream of Divine Light: Assists us with restoring spiritual freedom and with transformation of low vibrational energies and can empower us with the ability to forgive.

The violet divine light frequency is aligned with Archangel Zadkiel, whose name means "Righteousness of God."

The violet stream of divine light emanates directly from the cosmic sun of Absolute Love. This transformational cosmic frequency clears karmic energies and unforgiveness energy that can keep a place, person, or object energetically tied to nonbeneficial patterns. Archangel Zadkiel or the violet light (or both) works to transmute and transform any low vibrational energies into higher vibrational energies. Archangel Zadkiel and the violet light can help us overcome our most-traumatic life experiences and emotional pain. Violet light can restore our spiritual power and freedom from karmic ties and soul history patterns that keep repeating themselves so that we can go to the next level of spiritual growth.

How to Connect with Your Divine-Light-Clearing Team

To spiritually and energetically connect with your divine-light-clearing team, you must first prepare your energy vibration by setting the most optimal energetic atmosphere. You do this through the expansion of your heart and soul energy combined with clear-focused mental power. When unconditional love is the motivating factor in your energy-clearing work, then you will naturally form a strong, clear connection with your divine-light-clearing team. To work with your divine-light-clearing team, it is spiritually important for you to set a clear intention and request to receive universal support in all of your energy-clearing work. The following exercise is created to help you safely connect with universal support and spiritually invite your divine-light-clearing team to assist you. Setting a clear intention is a spiritual invitation for them to cocreate with you for all of your energy-clearing and healing purposes. The creative steps of the exercise will help you shift your energy vibration into a powerful balanced resonance for spiritual support.

Prepare Your Energy Exercise

A Template Pattern to Prepare for Your Energy-Clearing Work

Use this creative template and energy exercise to help you prepare and empower your personal energy vibration, ready to begin your energy-clearing treatments. It will help you set the correct energetic atmosphere to align with the universal support of your divine-light-clearing team.

Step 1: Set a Clear Mental Intention

"I intend to connect with my divine-light-clearing team of universal support to help me in all of my energy-clearing work for the greatest good of myself and all concerned."

Step 2: Expand Your Heart Energy

Begin to align your consciousness with loving thoughts and happy memories that invoke radiant joy. This simple step immediately helps you naturally expand your heart energy by shifting your overall vibration into a higher elevated expression of light. You will then help generate the spiritual frequency to connect with the higher vibrational forces of your Absolute Love, universal support, and divine-light-clearing team. Through doing steps 1 and 2 you instantly help balance your soul's light within your heart energy center, which is a cosmic portal of love and light. To shift it up another vibrational gear, begin to align with the feeling of gratitude and thankfulness for your life and for the universal support that is always available to you. The spiritual power generated by gratitude is what amplifies your soul's creative power. Now that you have created the right energetic atmosphere for yourself, you can begin with the all-important cosmic polarities.

Step 3: Cosmic Polarities

This spiritually powerful step is what will connect your body, mind, and soul energy with the cosmic polarities of Mother Earth and Father Heaven energy. By connecting to Mother Earth energy, you help ground your soul's light with the nurturing and life-giving energy of planet Earth, which not only protects you as you do your energy-clearing work but also provides the nurturing feminine energy through your energy-clearing treatments. By connecting to Father Heaven energy, you help expand your soul's light with the creative force of cosmic consciousness, which spiritually protects you as you do your energy-clearing work. It also helps provide the masculine energy of cosmic polarity through your energy-clearing treatments. To begin this easy step, you activate your creative imagination and visualization. Visualize a ball of dazzling gold light sitting within the center of your heart chakra. Expand the light so that it grows bigger than your physical body and you find that you are emerged within a force field of golden light. Focus back on your heart chakra and direct a stream of golden light moving in both directions, upward and out into the cosmos, and downward into the center of Mother Earth. Imagine the golden light moving upward, going through your throat chakra, third-eye chakra, and crown chakra and then exiting out of your crown chakra while continuing to move up high into the cosmos until you reach a brilliant golden sun or star. You connect your soul's light into this golden sun, which is where you connect with universal support and draw down the celestial frequencies in all of your energy-clearing work. The golden sun is symbolic of Absolute Love and is where all the divine light frequencies of creation emerge, which then emanate their light rays through the universal support of archangels and benevolent light beings. Now imagine the golden light moving downward from your heart chakra, going through your solar plexus chakra, sacral plexus chakra, and base chakra, and then continue to move the golden light down through your legs and exiting out of the soles of your feet. Move this golden light all the way into the center of Mother Earth, where you will connect your soul's light into a pinkish-silver sphere of light. This is where you connect to the life-giving energy of Mother Earth, which grounds and supports your physical body as you align with the higher vibrational realms of light. Cosmic polarities provide extraordinary creative power and spiritual protection. State the following once you have connected your soul's light to the energies of heaven and earth.

Step 4: Invite and Thank Universal Support

Now that you have followed all four steps and you are cosmically aligned, you simply request the assistance for universal support. State the following: "I request unlimited universal support to always assist me every time I do my energy-clearing work. I willingly choose to cocreate beneficial outcomes with my divine-light-clearing team. Thank you [state gratitude to whom you want to include in your divine light team] to the seven archangels of divine light, my guardian angel, spirit guides, spirit doctors, and my spirit family for joining forces with my soul's light for the good of all."

CHAPTER 7

ENERGY MEASUREMENT
(ENERGY TESTING/DOWSING)

There are more things in heaven and earth, Horatio, than are
dreamt of in your philosophy.

—SHAKESPEARE

When it comes to doing an energy-clearing treatment for a home, a person, or even an object, we can actually measure the overall energy vibration of whatever it is we've decided to energetically clear before we begin, and then once again afterward. Not only does this enable us to discern potential energy problems, it also offers us a way to observe tangible improvements of the energetic adjustments made during the treatment when measured again afterward. Energy testing is a process used by many professionals such as chiropractors and kinesiologists. Kinesiology, also known as biomechanics, is the study of body movement, and applied kinesiology (AK) uses muscle testing to test the strength or weakness of muscles as a form of diagnosis and treatment. Donna Eden, bestselling author of *Energy Medicine*, has taken muscle testing to a whole new level. She states that energy testing can be learned quickly, and you don't need any great intuitive powers or the ability to "see energies." With energy testing, you can reliably assess, in any given moment, the body's unique energies and energy fields and their ever-oscillating fluctuations. Eden also mentions that she prefers the term "energy test" to the more common term "muscle test," to emphasize that the objective of the test is to determine not the strength of a muscle but rather how the body's energies are flowing through it.

Chiropractor Bradley Nelson, the bestselling author of *The Emotion Code*, explains how energy testing can help us get to the origin of a problem. When it comes to the energy-clearing aspect of the work, Dr. Nelson uses a magnet to help clear the energetic disturbances. He has created a chart of emotions to discern if their specific energy frequencies are trapped within the body and energy systems. Trapped emotions can cause an array of symptomatic problems. Each trapped emotion can be energy-tested and then energetically cleared as a way to help the body and mind rebalance. In his fascinating book, he tells the story of how he helped a patient of his heal from chest pain and difficulty breathing when he cleared the trapped emotion of heartache from her. After checking on her vital signs and finding them to be normal, Dr. Nelson energy-tested her body to see if these physical symptoms were being caused by a trapped emotion, and the answer he got from her body was "yes." He continued to test his patient for the specific trapped emotion and quickly determined that it was heartache. He then went on to clear it from her, which resulted in the chest pain leaving and her breathing returning to a normal rhythm. This is the extraordinary power of energy-clearing work and is also the reason why healers, energy experts, and other kinds of alternative therapies are just as invaluable in their service to others as medical doctors and medical treatment are. This is because we are body, mind, and soul, and when imbalances and health issues arise, they are not always going to be resolved with physical body diagnosis and the best medicine, and especially so for people with chronic, long-term, persisting issues and for those whom doctors are unable to find and alleviate the root cause. Everyone in their dedicated service of helping another heal, no matter if it's the traditional orthodox way, psychiatry, or psychology, or via a spiritual path and healer of some kind, is truly needed. The divine source works its splendor through medical science just as it does through the heart and hands of a healer. It is judging another way as being less efficient that we will limit our own path and potential.

Barbara Brennan is a pioneer and innovator in the field of energy consciousness and is a former NASA physicist who has dedicated her life to exploring the human energy field and the realms of human consciousness. In her extraordinary book, *Hands of Light*, Brennan discusses the use of energy testing with a pendulum, in order to measure the energy of the chakras and to discern any malfunction. Both Brennan and Nelson are experts in the body's energy systems, and energy testing is just one significant way to discern energy problems and measure energy flow and strength. Within this exciting chapter you will learn how to energy-test by dowsing with a pendulum in order to measure the overall energy of a property, person, or object, so that you can gain deeper insight into any energy problems. However, you are also going to go one step further with the pendulum than just the process of energy testing—you are also going to discover how to use the pendulum as a great tool for energy-clearing treatments. By doing so, you will be able to make any necessary energetic adjustments through the energy-clearing process to help restore greater energetic harmony and flow. You will then be able to retest and measure the overall energy vibration once more of whatever it is you are energetically treating, to see if there are any significant improvements. I will guide you through the exact steps to measure energy with the use of a pendulum and then to clear energy. You will then discover how to clear the energy of homes, people, animals, and objects, which will be covered in the oncoming chapters.

Energy measurement with a pendulum is an amazing biofeedback tool that, with regular practice, will enable you to become more confident and proficient in its use. Practice will also deepen your ability to intuitively discern different kinds of energetic disturbances, since your intuition will become more expansive. Plus, you will become adept at using the pendulum to make the necessary energetic corrections and adjustments required to help restore balance, harmony, and energetic equilibrium back to a person, animal, home, or object. Your energy-clearing journey starts with the art of pendulum dowsing as a way of receiving information.

Dowsing

Dowsing is an ancient practice best known as water divining or water witching. The dowsers would be asked to locate the best place to drill to find a water well and would use a forked stick, often from the branches of an old peach tree, and go out in the fields to locate underground water. The oldest record of dowsing showing human figures holding forked sticks is said to be the pictographs on the walls of the Tassili Caves in South Algeria, dating from around 6,000 BCE. However, in *The Pendulum Book*, by Hanna Kroeger,[10] she writes that the oldest known picture of dowsing was found in the ruins of ancient Mesopotamia in 1300 BCE, where a priest is pictured using a forked divining rod. Hanna Kroeger was a remarkable woman who's lovingly remembered as the "Grandmother of Health." Her work with the pendulum in service of helping others to heal is legendary. In *The Pendulum Book*, Hanna remarks that if you are injured in the wilderness, there is help within a 300-foot circumference of the place where you are hurt. There is a plant, a flower, or a root to be placed on your injury. Stay calm, employ your pendulum, and let God show you the way. A pilot had heard about Hanna's lectures with the pendulum. One evening he came into trouble when flying a single-engine plane, and he had an accident in icy conditions away from civilization. He calmed down and prayed, remembered what Hanna had said, and he said, "Okay, I will find help." In the snow he marked the directions north, south, east, and west. Then he took his key as a pendulum and asked the Lord for help. Slowly the pendulum showed northeast. He asked of the pendulum how many steps? It counted 165. The man dragged his injured feet the distance and found shelter from ice and snow in a cavern, which was thickly covered with pine needles and dry leaves. He was recovered the next day without having received any frostbite or further injuries.

Dowsing is becoming increasingly popular in the present day, with specialized niches that include health dowsing and map dowsing to locate missing persons or objects and dowsing for technological and geopathic stress. "To dowse," says Christopher Bird, bestselling author of *The Divining Hand*,[11] "is to search with the aid of a handheld instrument such as a forked stick or a pendular bob on the end of a string—for anything: subterranean water flowing in a narrow underground fissure, a pool of oil or a vein of mineral ore, a buried sewer pipe or electrical cable, an airplane downed in a mountain wilderness, a disabled ship helplessly adrift in a gale, a lost wallet or dog, a missing person, perhaps a buried treasure." If you want to find out more about this fascinating art, Christopher Bird provides a complete history of the art of dowsing around the world and discusses in detail the various existing theories attempting to explain this extraordinary phenomenon.

In France, health dowsing became more prominent during the eighteenth century. The late Abbe Mermet was a country priest and had the satisfaction of being acclaimed during his lifetime as the "King of Dowsers," not only in France but all over the continent of Europe. He studied and developed the natural sensitivity of the human organism to radiations and force fields, applying his knowledge with attested success to the discovery of gold, water, disease, and missing persons, and to the solving of all kinds of problems. His important classic on the principles and practice of radiesthesia raised it to the level of a new science.

Radiesthesia

Abbe Mermet was once contacted by a doctor whose child was apparently dying and not responding to any treatment. With his pendulum he immediately located the trouble in the region of the liver. Again, with seeking intuitive answers by using the pendulum, he established the fact that the infant's stomach could tolerate milk only provided it was diluted with water. The child then made a rapid recovery. The doctor, who like so many of his colleagues had ridiculed dowsers, now firmly believes in the pendulum as a valuable diagnostic instrument.

ENERGY MEASUREMENT SCALES AND CHARTS

David Hawkins developed a well-known map of consciousness (Hawkins 1995, *Power vs. Force*)[12] that pertained to a variety of man's problems. This map of consciousness developed out of a decade of research in a variety of energy fields. Using a logarithmic scale, Hawkins calibrated the power of an energy field and its direction in consciousness, ranging from a state of low consciousness to the highest state of consciousness. The energy fields he determined to be low in consciousness do not support life, while those he determined to be high in consciousness do. The calibration of the energy fields starts at zero, and what the world calls enlightenment calibrates from 600 to 1000. Anything measured under 200 was deemed to be negative states, and anything above 200 was deemed to be positive states.

Hawkins used a simple system of muscle testing to test a person's energy in response to where they resonate on the map of consciousness. What this shows us is that anything with an energetic radiation can be measured. A pendulum can also be used as an energetic diagnostic tool to measure a person's emotional state, mental state, physical state, and overall level of vibration and consciousness. A pendulum can also be used to measure the energy level and condition of any place, environment, and object.

In Eugene Maurey's book *Exorcism*,[13] he writes about the following measure of evaluation with the use of a pendulum.

Bill Finch in his excellent thesis on spirit possession, *The Pendulum and Possession*,[14] created a yardstick to identify and classify a personality. The personality may be a living person or a spirit entity. The entity may be a possessing spirit. When an exorcist makes a positive identification of the type and strength of the invading spirits, he can be more effective by varying his approach to the exorcism. On a scale of minus thirty to plus thirty, a living person or spirit entity is analyzed. Zero energetically measured as a balanced mind and minus thirty energetically measured as a killer mind.

The Bovis Scale

The Bovis scale is named after a French researcher, Anton Bovis,[15] who studied the earth energies of the great pyramids in the 1930s. The Bovis scale is used to measure natural earth energies, with ranges running from zero to infinity. The scale measures positive and negative energy, which can be thought of as beneficial and nonbeneficial. In the Bovis scale, if the object being measured is from 0 to 6,500, this is considered to be in the negative range and is not beneficial. If the object being measured shows a range of 6,500 and above, the object is radiating more positive energy that will be more beneficial.

THE PENDULUM

A pendulum is a weighted object on a string, and while almost anything can be used for this purpose, such as a ring on a piece of thread, there are also uniquely designed pendulums that are created with geometric patterns said to produce healing radiations. However, for simple dowsing purposes such as yes and no answers, any weighted object on a string will be sufficient. In this sense you can easily make your own pendulum, or you can purchase one of your own personal preference, since they range in price from being very reasonable to those that are in the hundreds of dollars. My first pendulum was a rose quartz crystal pendulum that worked perfectly fine for me even though some dowsers and pendulum healers don't rate them. This is often because crystals need energy clearing since they absorb energy. I found it to be very sufficient, and to me it's been one of my favorite ones. Rose quartz is a beautiful healing crystal that aligns with the heart energy and with the Archangel Chamuel's divine healing-light frequency. I now have several different pendulums, and I honestly don't find one to be stronger than another. However, pendulum experts say certain ones give off powerful healing energies due to the design and makeup of the pendulum and due to the geometric shape being created in its vortex of energy as it spins in clearing or harmonizing mode. As a pendulum spins, it is said that the length of time it spins, and the velocity of the spin, is what it takes and is needed to clear some kind of imbalance. This means that some spins will be faster than others, and some will last longer than others in their duration. I've found that when a pendulum is in clearing mode and something significant is shifting, then it does increase in speed, but not always in its length of time. It can also be a relatively short, fast spin, which then stops once the specific request and work are done. In this book, pendulum clearing and healing (rebalancing) work begins and ends with universal support and divine light assistance. Through prayer commands that set the pendulum to move via the nervous system of the body, the energy vortex created from the pendulum spin is amplified by the divine light power and is what generates transformational shifts in whatever is being cleared. This is the art of cocreation, since you aren't doing it in your own power, but you are joining forces with the magnified power of universal Light. This also serves to protect your energy from energetic fatigue, since universal intelligence takes the lead in helping you clear energy and restore equilibrium.

Pendulum Movements

Now it's time to start working with the pendulum and to understand its movements. You can use either hand to hold the pendulum, yet most people will use the hand that they write with. Hold the string of the pendulum between your thumb and index finger, leaving around 3 to 4 inches between your hand and the pendulum. Store any excess string in the palm of your hand so that it doesn't dangle down and interfere with any movements. Let's begin with the following steps to help you establish your own personal pattern:

Step 1: Connect with Your Pendulum

If it's your first time holding a pendulum, then it's a good idea to hold the pendulum within each palm in order to get a feel for it as it vibrationally connects with your personal energy. Each time that you energetically connect with and use your pendulum, the greater vibrational sync you will establish with it. Now begin to swing the pendulum back and forth to get a feel for the weight of the pendulum and its movement. Next, simply hold the pendulum over and above your right knee, and you will soon find the pendulum will begin to swing on its own accord and will typically move in a clockwise direction. This is because the energy polarity of the right knee tends to move in a clockwise direction. Now try holding the pendulum over and above your left knee, and you will again see the pendulum move on its own, typically in a counterclockwise direction. If your directions are switched, it can simply be because you are overly tired or dehydrated (or both). When our energies are dehydrated, they tend to run backward. Have a glass of water and take four deep, slow breaths, in through your nose and out of your mouth, to help you rebalance,

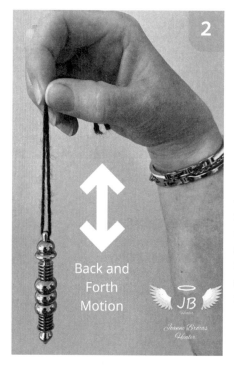

and try the experiment once more. If you are still switched, then it can also be because this is the unique way that your own energy currently pulsates. In this case, then you will know that it's fine to continue. Being energetically switched in our body's polarities can affect our dowsing accuracy.

Step 2: Establish a Yes Movement

When you are ready, you are going to ask the pendulum to show you a "yes" movement. This is typically a vertical swing back and forth. If you don't get any movement, you can simply swing it back and forth vertically while you assign it to be your yes movement. Your intuitive mind will remember this.

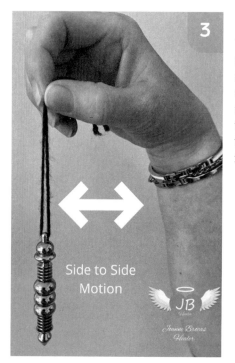

Step 3: Establish a No Movement

When you are ready, you are going to ask the pendulum to show you a "no" movement. This is typically a horizontal swing side to side. If you don't get any movement, you can simply swing it side to side horizontally while you assign it to be your no movement. Your intuitive mind will remember this.

Step 4: Energy–Clearing Movement

When you are ready, you are going to ask the pendulum to show you the energy-clearing movement. This is typically a counterclockwise direction as your pendulum swings in a circular motion. If you don't get any movement, you can simply swing it in a counterclockwise direction (to the left), while you assign it to be your "clearing" movement. Your intuitive mind will remember this.

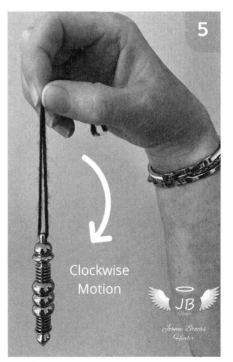

Step 5: Energy–Harmonizing Movement

When you are ready, you are going to ask the pendulum to show the energy-harmonizing movement. This is typically a clockwise direction as your pendulum swings in a circular motion. If you don't get any movement, you can simply swing it in a clockwise direction (to the right), while you assign it to be your "harmonizing" movement. Your intuitive mind will remember this.

You've now learned the four main energy movements in which you will be working with to test (yes and no answers), to measure energy (chart), and to clear and balance energy (counterclockwise and clockwise movements).

USING A PENDULUM TO MEASURE ENERGY

You can use the following energy measurement chart to dowse with a pendulum to determine the overall rate of vibration and the general energetic condition of what you decide to clear. Whether you choose to include the pendulum as a tool in your energy-clearing work is one of personal preference, since you will still be able to adapt and use the energy-clearing protocols in the following chapters in order to participate in energy-clearing treatments. However, the pendulum will help you focus your mind and synchronize your brain waves to empower your intuition as you access universal intelligence and benevolent cocreative assistance.

The energy measurement chart provides a simple way to discern the overall energy frequency of a place, a person, a pet, an object, etc., helping you detect and discern the difference between a range of low- and high-vibe frequencies. When measuring the overall energy of a house, person, pet, or object, typically anything measuring between 75 and 100 percent falls into the "high vibe/healthy" range, meaning that the overall energy vibrations of what's being measured are already in pretty good shape and will require a minimal amount of energy clearing. In this sense, when you go through the energy-clearing protocol with the pendulum (chapter 8), it may spin for only a short period of time (seconds), and some steps may not be required at all. Anything measuring between 50 and 75 percent falls into the "strong vibe/positive" range and generally indicates energetic residue and

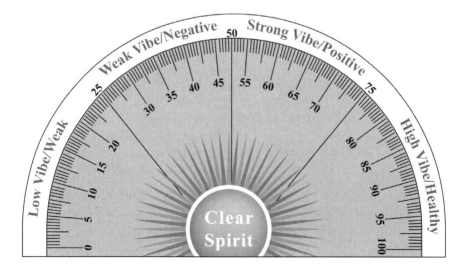

imbalances, yet nothing overly problematic. The closer the measurement of something leans toward 75 percent, the higher vibrational strength it will resonate. Anything measuring between 25 and 50 percent falls into the "weak-vibe/negative" range and generally indicates that what's being measured has sufficient energetic concerns at this time. When going through the energy-clearing protocol, the pendulum may take much longer when in clearing mode, spinning for maybe a minute or so at a time. Further energy-clearing treatments will probably also be required until the overall energy of what's being cleared eventually shifts into higher vibrational resonance and balance and then continues to hold that balance. This is because beneficial energetic shifts will hold and maintain their higher vibrational resonance for only so long when there are still preexisting energetic concerns with the property that often require more time to be fully resolved. Anything measuring from 0 to 25 percent falls into the "low-vibe/negative" range and generally indicates an accumulation of energy problems or one main and critical issue. These problems and issues can be due to negative house memories and energy patterns, probable spiritual interference, and the likes of geopathic stress. However, if you asked if it is okay for you to proceed with the house energy-clearing treatment and you got a yes response from the pendulum, then all you need to do is to go through the protocol, applying each step to make the necessary energetic adjustments, and you will surely help the overall energy of the home to shift, lift, and increase in its vibrational resonance. You are always working with unlimited universal support to help you, and you aren't doing it in your own creative power. When a home's vibration is significantly low and in the negative range (it will never be 0 percent), it can mean that the people who live in the home are also experiencing energetic concerns and life struggles. In the next chapter you will use the energy measurement chart with your pendulum and ask to be shown the overall energy of the home prior to you beginning a house energy-clearing treatment. You will take note of the measurement, and after the treatment has finished you will remeasure the overall energy of the property to notice any tangible improvements.

Now that you've been introduced to the movements of the pendulum plus the energy measurement chart, it's time to move on to part 3 of the book, where you will put all of this into practice to begin your first energy-clearing treatment.

PART 3

ENERGY-CLEARING SOLUTIONS

(STEPS AND PROTOCOLS)

CHAPTER 8

HOUSE ENERGY-CLEARING TREATMENT
(STEPS AND PROTOCOL)

If you hear a voice within you say, "You cannot paint," then by all means paint, and that voice will be silenced.

—Vincent van Gogh

It's time to begin the process and application of a house energy-clearing treatment. In this practical yet exciting chapter, you will be guided through the exact steps and protocol required to successfully complete a house energy-clearing treatment. This energetic process will help restore balance and harmony back to the overall atmosphere of the home environment, which will also help support the personal energies of all who reside there. This important chapter is one that you can return back to again and again until the house energy-clearing protocol becomes second nature. In the next chapter you will also find out how to do two different kinds of long-distance house energy-clearing treatments.

Apply your intuition and be creative as you move through the house energy-clearing protocol. If you feel that you want to leave anything out or you want to add something in, then feel free to do so. These steps I give you formulate a solid foundation that has unlimited creative potential for further expansion. Trust your intuition and use the steps and protocol as a way to springboard right into your own unique style of house energy-clearing work.

House Energy-Clearing Treatment

When doing a house or any other energy-clearing treatment, it's always best to do so when you feel that you are emotionally balanced, and when you know that you won't be interrupted. Note: If you don't want to use a pendulum to energy-test, measure energy, or help clear energy, then you can simply use the necessary energy-clearing prayer commands found in the protocol section, combined with your intuition. When approaching an energy clearing in this way and you are unsure if something needs clearing and adjusting, then all you need to remember is that because you are working in cocreation with benevolent universal support—whenever you ask for something to be energetically cleared when it doesn't need to be, then you won't be interfering with the energy of the place. In other words, the spiritual support system will always work in harmony with the highest and best energetic outcome and will prevent any unnecessary changes from taking place if not required. Some energy patterns resonating within an environment or within a person will be held in place for a higher purpose until they are ready to be transformed, processed, and energetically cleared.

Prior to beginning the house energy-clearing treatment, make a note of how many people live in the home, their names, and their ages. This will help you understand the energetic mix of people's combined vibrational frequencies (chapter 1). Plus, you can offer to do a personal energy-clearing treatment for anyone who may require it (chapter 11) to help them harmonize with the new elevated vibration resonating within the home environment due to the house energy-clearing treatment. Also make a note of how many pets live in the home. Are they healthy? Again, you can offer to do an energy-clearing treatment for them separately if required to help support and empower them.

Here are the exact steps explaining all about the house energy-clearing treatment, followed by the protocol of energy-clearing prayer commands and instructions to help you successfully complete a house energy-clearing treatment.

House Energy–Clearing Steps

Step 1: Energetic Protection and Connection Prayer (Cocreation)

Always begin with a prayer for energetic protection and for spiritual connection to help you connect with and direct the universal clearing/healing forces of Divine Love and Light. You will find the prayers that I use in the "House Energy-Clearing Protocol" section, yet you are welcome to adjust these to your own style and belief system. When doing an energy-clearing treatment for someone else's home, it is always best to ask their permission to do so, just in case they don't want you changing and rearranging the energetic atmosphere of their home environment. We must always be spiritually mindful of energy-clearing work and getting involved in situations that we have no business interfering with.

You've already discovered how to utilize prayer power from chapter 6. Whenever you pray, remember to do so from an expanded heart energy so that you will set the correct energetic frequency prior to beginning any energy-clearing treatment. Expanding your heart energy enables your soul to tap into greater creative potential and spiritual power residing within you and within the universe. Practicing the prayer power meditations in chapter 6 will continue to help boost your creative prayer power and heighten your intuition. Relaxing your body and your mind is also going to help you more easily align with your universal spiritual support system of guides, angels, and expert benevolent helpers. Expansive heart energy and consciousness indicates that you are open to receive universal support, and you aren't doing the energy-clearing work in your own limited creative power—which is what can lead to limited results or temporary energetic fatigue.

Step 2: Energy Test to Check If You Can Begin

You will be using the pendulum to ask aloud if it is appropriate to proceed with a house energy-clearing treatment for "this house." If the pendulum swings back and forth in the yes position, then you will know that it is appropriate to proceed. You don't need to make it any more difficult than this. If the answer is no, then it's not appropriate to proceed at this time, so don't do it. As previously mentioned in chapter 7, reasons for a no response, showing that it's not appropriate to proceed with an energy-clearing treatment at this time, can be because you are dehydrated, you are overly tired (your energies may have switched polarities), or you may lack confidence in your ability to do so, or it can simply be because the energy of the place doesn't require an energy clearing at this specific time. Have a glass of water to rehydrate, do an energy-balancing technique (chapter 7), and ask again, or simply leave it and ask again at a different time. What if you still get a no response from the pendulum when asking again if it is appropriate to proceed? Then you can start with an energy-clearing treatment for yourself as a way to help you become familiarized with energy-clearing treatments. It is very rare that you will continually get a no response when preparing to do a house energy-clearing treatment, since even if you don't get to clear everything as mentioned in the steps provided, you will still get to clear some of them. At times a repeated no response from the pendulum can simply mean that "at this time" someone with more experience in energy-clearing work is required to assist in this particular space. Since you are beginning with your own home environment, this is probably not going to be the case for you. An example may be if you are asking to clear the energy of a place that has too much spiritual interference, of which you may not have enough understanding of (just yet). In this case, you would receive a continuous no response or you simply wouldn't be guided to energetically clear such a home in the first place. The universe gives you only what you are ready and able to cope with and are responsible enough to deal with. Therefore, you can leave any fear you have at bay and proceed in your house energy-clearing treatment with excitement and delight at this whole new world of energetic resonance opening up to you. As you continue in your energy-clearing practice and in your prayer power meditations (chapter 6), you will increasingly build your confidence, will amplify your intuition, and will empower your energy-clearing skills. If you don't want to use a pendulum to energy-test to check if it's appropriate for you to proceed, then you can either do a sway test or a finger test or simply just rely on your intuition for a yes/no response. I find the pendulum to be the fastest and easiest method of dowsing and energy testing, and it's an excellent feedback device for our intuition.

Step 3: Measure the Overall Energy of the Home

Use the energy measurement chart (chapter 7) with your pendulum and ask to be shown the overall energy of the home. The energy measurement chart provides a simple way to discern the overall energy frequency of a place, a person, a pet, an object, etc., helping you detect and discern the difference between a range of low- and high-vibe frequencies. When measuring the overall energy of the house, typically anything measuring between 75 and 100 percent falls into the "high-vibe/ healthy" range, meaning that the overall energy vibrations of what's being measured are already in pretty good shape and will require a minimal amount of energy clearing. In this sense, when you go through the energy-clearing steps with the pendulum, it may spin for only a short period of time (seconds), and some steps may not be required at all. Anything measuring between 50 and 75 percent falls into the "strong vibe/positive" range and generally indicates energetic residue and imbalances, yet nothing overly problematic. The closer the measurement of something leans toward 75 percent, the higher vibrational strength it will resonate. Anything measuring between 25 and 50 percent falls into the "weak-vibe/negative" range and generally indicates that the house has sufficient energetic concerns at this time. When going through the energy-clearing protocol, the pendulum may take much longer when in clearing mode, spinning for maybe a minute or so at a time. Further house energy-clearing treatments will probably also be required until the overall energy of the home eventually shifts into higher vibrational resonance and balance and then continues to hold that balance. This is because beneficial energetic shifts will hold and maintain their higher vibrational resonance for only so long when there are still preexisting energetic concerns with the property that often require more time to be fully resolved. Anything measuring from 0 to 25 percent falls into the "low-vibe/negative" range and generally indicates an accumulation of energy problems or one main and critical issue. These problems and issues can be due to negative house memories and energy patterns, probable spiritual interference, and the likes of geopathic stress. However, if you asked if it is okay for you to proceed with the house energy-clearing treatment and you got a yes response from the pendulum, then all you need to do is to go through the protocol, applying each step to make the necessary energetic adjustments, and you will surely help the overall energy of the home to shift, lift, and increase in its vibrational resonance. You are always working with unlimited universal support to help you, and you aren't doing it in your own creative power. When a home's vibration is significantly low and in the negative range (it will never be 0 percent), it can mean that the people who live in the home are also experiencing energetic concerns and life struggles. After a house energy-clearing treatment, it is therefore also a good idea for them to experience personal energy-clearing treatments in order to help them harmonize their personal energies with the new elevated energy frequency now resonating within the home's environment. When the home's energy and the people's energies become more coherent with higher vibrational energies, improvements can take root and begin to blossom. Beneficial changes can then occur in people's health, relationships, finances, work life, and life circumstances, which are the combined results of internal and external shifts in consciousness and vibration. If you don't want to use a pendulum and chart to measure the overall energetic frequency of the place, then just trust and rely on your intuition to discern how the overall energy within the home feels to you.

Step 4: Choose a Room to Begin and Discern Potential Energy Problems

Now that you've prepared your energy (expanded heart), prayed for spiritual protection and support, asked if it's appropriate to proceed and got a yes response, and also measured the overall energy of the home so that when you remeasure later you will be able to notice any tangible improvements, it's now time to choose a room to begin your house energy-clearing treatment. You can start anywhere you like or wherever you are intuitively drawn to start. When you first enter the room you've chosen, walk to a space that you find comfortable to begin your energy-clearing work. It doesn't matter if this is in the middle of the room or near a corner, etc., as long as you leave the necessary space surrounding you to use your pendulum to make energetic adjustments. If you feel more comfortable sitting down, then this is fine, since comfort will help you feel more relaxed. I typically always stand when I do energy-clearing treatments, yet it's one of personal preference.

Now that you are in the room you've chosen, it is time to discern the overall energy of this space. You don't need to measure the overall energy of the room with your pendulum and chart unless you really want to, because one measurement taken of the overall energy of the home before you begin is sufficient, and it will save you plenty of time. Also, when you begin to discern the energy of a small space with your intuitive faculties, you will help develop and fine-tune your psychic senses of clairvoyance, clairaudience, and clairsentience, among others. Become intuitively aware of what you begin to energetically sense and feel within the room. You can use a notebook to jot down information that you want to remember and deal with later, when making further energetic adjustments. Ask yourself the following questions to help activate your intuition: If the room could speak to you, what personality and character does it have? Does it emanate joy, sadness, loneliness, fear, etc.? Does the overall energy of the room feel busy, noisy, chaotic, quiet, still, or even lifeless?

Now it's time to make a note of any areas of clutter, any dark spaces, or anything broken, leaking, or in need of general repair. If so, these are aspects of the room that need to be physically adjusted in order to help support the overall energetic balance of that particular space. Check each corner of the room to see how congested they are with clutter or if there is any furniture located there, then make sure that there is no clutter on the furniture, such as stacks of paperwork or other items that can be easily stored away. Congested corners will begin to accumulate energy that can stagnate, and then the rest of the space will begin to lack decent energetic flow. Also check whether windows and doors close properly. Windows spiritually symbolize eyes of the soul and the ability to see things from a higher perspective. Cracked windows, dirty windows, and windows that have been painted so they're shut tight can reflect both spiritual and physical imbalance with perception and with eye issues. Doors that don't close properly or that don't open fully into the room due to them being obstructed with items of furniture or clutter, especially the external doors of the home, front and back, will interfere with energy being able to enter into a space. Next, check the ceiling of the room. Are there any exposed overhead beams? These can cause an energetic disturbance that can interfere with sleep patterns if located within the bedroom, and with our moods and mental focus if located elsewhere. If the bed or work desk can easily be moved somewhere that is less exposed within the room, then this is a good idea. If not, an energy clearing of the room can help prevent the adverse energetic effects of the beams impinging upon those who spend time there.

Notice to see if there is any building work or decorating being done within the room. Also, what color are the walls of the room? Remember that colors emit specific energetic frequencies that can influence the personal energy fields of people. Refer back to chapter 5 for information about colors within the home environment and their influence on us. Maybe there is a color theme within the bedroom that is bright yellow, which stimulates the nervous system and can keep the mind alert, interfering with relaxation and sleep. The color yellow would be more appropriate for a home office or a kitchen. Noticing things like this can help you make decisions about making specific changes to the room or for offering beneficial suggestions to a loved one or friend when doing a house energy-clearing treatment for them.

Finally, make a note of what purpose the room is assigned to and is being used for: a bedroom, a kitchen, an office, a spare room, etc. The reason for this is that every room has its own purpose and unique vibrational frequency. The energy of an office is a far different frequency from the energy of a bedroom. Therefore, if the bedroom is being used as a bedroom-come-office space, then both of these energetic atmospheres impinge on each other and make the overall harmony of the space chaotic. In this case, if the main purpose of the room does indeed need to be shared with other assigned spaces due to a lack of overall square footage, then establishing energetic equilibrium with each other will help create a blended balance. However, it's always best to keep the bedroom as one assigned space if that's an option.

Now that you've intuitively discerned the overall energy of the room and you've taken notes of any physical interference, you will have gained valuable insight into what needs to be addressed within this particular space. You can go back to the space at a later date to make the necessary physical adjustments and corrections.

The next step is going to be your first energy-clearing command!

Step 5: Clear the Etheric Energy of the Room

This aspect of the energy clearing addresses clearing the original design and structure of the room, any further additions to the structure (building work/ extensions), any decorating being done to the room, the etheric purpose of the room, and any shared purposes. It will also help clear any nonbeneficial energy resonating within the physical structure (substances/fabric) of the room that may adversely affect the overall energy of the room. You will be doing one energy-clearing command in the protocol section for all of this. Remember you are cocreating this energy-clearing command with your universal backup support system, which amplifies the creative power of your intention and instruction. You are connecting with and directing the universal forces of Creation.

Step 6: Clear the Emotional Energy of the Room

This aspect of the energy clearing addresses clearing any imbalanced emotional charges, which can range rom very recent to those that have accumulated over longer periods of time. Sadness, depression, anxiety, overwhelm, guilt, anger, frustration, and irritation, among many others, all leave their emotional imprints and energetic residue within the atmosphere of the home. Some rooms will experience less emotional stress than others. Clearing the emotional-energy charges emanating within a room also addresses clearing the emotional history of that space, originating from others who may have lived in the home and who shared that space before you.

Step 7: Clear the Mental Energy of the Room

This aspect of the energy clearing addresses clearing the creative expressed charges of any imbalanced thoughts, images, and visions due to the misdirected use of our powerful imagination and ego mind. This is often due to us worrying and obsessing over certain life challenges, worrying about our loved ones, and stressing about the future and what may be. Angry words spoken due to arguments can also create nonbeneficial mental residue within the home. Quarreling and anger can cause a very heavy atmosphere due to the emanation of nervous tension in the air. As the saying goes, you could cut the air with a knife. Our imagination and thought power can create images, shapes, and color that can appear within the energetic atmosphere of the room. Although invisible to our vision, these unseen energies can still adversely affect our personal energies and disposition. Clearing the mental residue of the room can bring the atmosphere of the room back to a level of inner peace and harmony so that our personal energies will be supported by a beneficial environment. Clearing the mental energy charges emanating within a room also addresses clearing the mental history of that space, originating from others who may have lived in the home and who shared that space before you.

Step 8: Clear the Spiritual Energies of the Room

This aspect of the energy clearing addresses clearing any imbalanced astral and spiritual energies such as unknown energetic anomalies, astral fragments, and spiritual interference that do not originate from this realm. The first of the four spiritual fields is associated with the heart and soul energy of the home, since it holds the energy frequencies of unconditional love, inner peace, and harmony. This heart and soul energy is what can support the family unit to stay harmonious and strong. When the heart and soul energy of the home is compromised by an overlay of congested energetic residue and other energetic imbalances, it lowers the property's overall vibrational frequency, affecting each room. The family unit can then become imbalanced, and the harmony between each other is disturbed.

The second of the four spiritual fields includes the property's perfect blueprint pattern of the property's original intent, purpose, and design. It is continuously projected to the etheric energy of the property to help spiritually and energetically sustain the physical form of the property. A home's purpose is to provide a safe haven for the family from the outside environment, such as from weather conditions and from any potential harm. There is also higher energetic maintenance and spiritual support from the next two spiritual fields, which help oversee the property and the family who live there. Part of this spiritual support is known as the guardian of the place/home. A low vibration of and within the property doesn't necessarily stop this support network; it simply weakens it. When this weakness happens, the property is made more vulnerable to astral and spiritual interference. Astral interference derives its energies from the lower astral realms, which is the closest in frequency to this dense world of matter. It can also include the psychic energy of the living (their misdirected thought forms). Such interference can manifest as persisting problems with the integrity of the property. Maybe when one issue is dealt with, another one quickly arises. Spiritual interference can be due to earthbound spirits taking residence, or other spiritual factors such as spiritual infestation (nonhuman entities). However, the latter is a minority and is typically associated with a property that's been used for black magic or one that has experienced a history of violence and abuse, which creates the energetic signature, invitation, and portal for such invisible detrimental interference. You will probably never encounter such a situation to clear, yet knowledge of why this happens is beneficial since it brings a greater understanding that eliminates any fearful perceptions.

Applying this energy-clearing command within a room is like removing invisible energetic debris that lacks the love vibration. Immediately the energy of the room can return to a more balanced and harmonious state. It's not that you are directly dealing with or removing earthbound spirits at this point in the protocol, yet if there are any within the room, you will be clearing their energetic spiritual residue. You will be shown how to address clearing and releasing spirit energies in step 12. This step, however, is such a simple command, and all it takes is your mental focus, concentration, and cocreation with the Light, and you will help restore the heart and soul energy of the home along with the guardian spirit of the home.

Step 9: Clear Any Objects and Items of Furniture

If you want to zone in on one object or one item of furniture at a time and do an energy clearing in this way, then this is totally fine. Otherwise, you can hold the mental intent that you are clearing all objects within the room or all items of furniture within the room that would benefit from an energy clearing. This is especially helpful if the room is brimming full of objects and furniture. Plus, not every object or item of furniture will require an energy clearing. Remember that you are clearing only nonbeneficial or low-vibe energies that do not support the overall energy of the room and the people who spend time there. If you do want to go ahead and clear one object or item of furniture at a time, then you can always dowse with the pendulum to ask if it requires an energy clearing. Just hold your pendulum a few inches above the object or item of furniture and ask, for example, "Does this dresser require an energy clearing today?" If you get a yes response, then great, go ahead and use the energy-clearing command over it or near to it. If you get a no response, then the object is fine just now and you can move on to something else.

However, if you are in the bedroom, then it is always a good idea to clear the energy of the bed separately. This is because of the hours of time people spend sleeping in beds, especially when all of their worries and fears come to the surface as they begin to relax. The more experience you gain with energy clearing, the more focused your mind can be to energy-clear all objects or items of furniture within the room. It is the power and strength of your intention and mental focus that enables you to generate more energy to cocreate with universal intelligence.

When doing an energy clearing on objects, furniture, jewelry, etc., remember that some of these items may be inherited, secondhand, or antique, and they can still carry the attachment energies of that particular time frame. In essence you will be helping clear the adverse energetic effects of other people's energies, thought forms, images, spiritual attachments, energy patterns, and emotional residue that may be absorbed into or attached to the object or item of furniture.

Step 10: Ask If There Is Any Geopathic Stress Adversely Affecting the Room

This step requires you to ask with the pendulum if there is any geopathic stress adversely affecting the room. If so, you will simply be clearing the adverse energetic effects of any geopathic stress interfering with the room.

Step 11: Ask If There Is Any Technological Stress Adversely Affecting the Room

Just like the previous step, you will ask with the pendulum if there is any technological stress adversely affecting the room. If so, you will clear the adverse energetic effects of any technological stress interfering with the room. This can be done as a collective energy-clearing command for the overall energy of the room, or you can decide to clear electrical appliances and items individually.

Step 12: Ask If There Are Any Ghost or Spirit Energies in the Room

Ghosts are nothing more than residual energy with pictures and sounds caught in time. They do not have consciousness and therefore they are unable to communicate with you. There is nothing to fear in clearing ghostly residue, plus remember you are working in cocreation with the Light (your divine clearing team and spiritual support system) for the good of all. Spirit energies can include attached fragmented soul energies that still have consciousness or actual spirit beings with active consciousness. Since you are working in harmony with your universal backup system, these spirits energies will be guided to the Spirit realm in the highest and best way, and any soul fragments will be returned to their source once energetically cleared. It is very important for any earthbound spirits to be released to the Spirit realm, since this is a far more suitable environment for their soul than that of the earth plane, which requires a dense body of matter to experience physical existence. I have helped countless spirit energies in this way, and over time I've discovered that as soon as they enter into their correct environment, they become full of Light, vibrant and joyful. Within the Light they are spiritually and energetically cleared of their earthly life residues that have previously weighed them down, impinging on both their rate of vibration and their consciousness. Since they are now free of earthly limitations, they will eventually feel spiritually free and unbounded. By staying within the physical dimension, they are unable to feel this way. It makes sense to help them regain their Light, joy, and spiritual renewal.

Spirit beings have free will, and sometimes they just don't want to go to the Spirit realm, and there can be many reasons for this. Yet, it is also important for the well-being of the home environment and for the family members that they move on. Even friendly spirits require an energy source, and because of this, all spirits tend to lower the overall energy of a house or person, even when this is unintentional. The universal support system will work in harmony with their free will for their greatest good and the good of the household. If they are adamant that they don't want to go to the Light, the benevolent spiritual help will greatly assist them and move them on to somewhere more appropriate until they are ready to continue on with their soul journey in the afterlife.

Within this step of the energy-clearing protocol, you won't be communicating with any earthbound spirits simply because there is no need for you to do so in order for you to best help them. You have nothing to fear when engaging in this step, because you are cocreating with universal intelligence. If you do encounter a spiritual issue that you feel you want more help with, then you can research and seek more-experienced assistance to help you. However, you really can clear and release the majority of earthbound spirit energies within this realm. It is very rare that you will ever encounter sinister spirit energies unless you are being guided to work in this unique genre. Such a genre can cover homes with spirit infestation, yet there is so much more to understand and learn about this complex yet fascinating subject, which is beyond the point and scope of this book. The book *Deadly Departed*, by my husband, Jock Brocas, covers deep insight into this area of spirit work.

Step 13: Ask If There Are Any Energy Patterns Adversely Affecting the Room

By clearing negative energy patterns at their point of origin, you will begin to help weaken and dissolve them.

Step 14: Raise the Level of Love Energy in the Room to the Highest Appropriate Level

This is an amazing "energy healing" command to use, since it helps integrate, process, and transform all the previous energy-clearing steps. While the previous steps will have already begun to raise the vibrational frequency of a room, by raising the level of love energy within the room it will help "seal the deal," so to speak. You are increasing the positive energy within the room to help sustain and maintain the results of the energy-clearing treatment.

The reason that you state, "Raise the level of love within this room to the highest appropriate level for the greatest good of all concerned," is because energy frequencies, whether extremely high or extremely low, can cause us physical discomfort depending on where our own personal vibration typically resonates. Stating for the greatest good of all concerned takes into account the personal energies of all family members, pets, and life force that occupy the space with you.

If you don't have time to go through all the energy-clearing commands in the protocol, then you can simply go ahead and raise the levels of love within each individual room of your home. This is similar to blessing the atmosphere of the room and house, yet the elevated frequency generated by the love energy may last for only so long until it drops once more. This is because there may be unresolved nonbeneficial energy factors still persisting there. Raising the level of love within a room, a place, a person, or a pet works very well and is super beneficial. However, if there are underlying energy problems, then it can be likened to taking a painkiller to mask the pain. When the medication wears off, the pain is still there. In this case, there will be temporary benefits and further energy-clearing work to do to help the love energy maintain its high vibrational frequency for longer periods of time. Eventually, though, the energy of a place and person does drop again because, let's face it, we are continually impressing our thoughts and emotions upon matter, and other people can impress their imbalanced energies upon our own. This is why regular home energy-clearing treatments are very beneficial. You can find out when you are ready to do the next clearing treatment by checking on the energy measurement chart to see if one is required. I typically check on the overall energy of my home environment every two months or so and then make the necessary energetic adjustments as required. In the meantime, you can always use step 14 to raise the level of love within each room of the home to the highest appropriate level for the greatest good of all concerned. After the final step of the house energy-clearing treatment, you will again discover the energy-healing command to use to help raise the level of love energy within all people and pets who live in the home. This important final command will greatly support the house energy-clearing treatment and will empower the personal energy fields of all people and pets who live in the home.

Julie found the perfect new home for herself and was looking forward to her move. The previous owner had lived there for many years and decided to relocate. I was asked by Julie if I could clear the energy of the home prior to her moving in. I did this as a distant energy-clearing treatment by using the full address of the home to help me spiritually and energetically zone into the vibration of the property. As I measured the energy of the home, it was significantly low. When a home is very low it's often a sign of spirit energies resonating there, although this is not always the case, and when I asked if there were any ghostly residue or spirit energies to clear, my pendulum response was a strong no. I went through my list of energy-clearing commands and reached steps 13 and 14, "clearing any negative energy patterns" and "raising the level of love energy within the home." This time for both commands, my pendulum spun wild. First it moved in a counterclockwise direction as it cleared the adverse energetic effects of negative energy patterns within the home. Then it began moving in a clockwise direction and was going at quite a speed when I asked that the level of love energy within the home be raised to the highest appropriate level. At the same time, I intuitively became aware of a deep sadness resonating within the home that was locked into the atmosphere there. Eventually my pendulum stopped to signify that the home had reached the appropriate level of love energy for the good of all concerned. I then finished the final steps of the home energy-clearing treatment, and I remeasured the overall energy of the home to check on any noticeable improvements. The overall energy of the home had certainly increased, and the home felt ready and welcoming for its next occupant. I spoke with Julie about the sadness I'd intuitively felt within the home. Julie told me that the previous owner had lost his wife three years previously after many years of her being sick. This made sense, since the negative energy patterns in a place can involve patterns of sickness, illness, and disease. The sadness I'd intuitively felt was connected to the man's grief from the loss of his wife, which was palpable to the home's energetic atmosphere. If Julie had moved in without the home being energetically prepared and rebalanced, then she may have become emotionally influenced and triggered by the palpable sadness resonating there. The energy patterns of illness could also generate concerns about her own health and well-being at times that she felt unwell. However, this is not always the case. Julie has a joyful disposition, and moving into a home that's been energetically prepared for her will help her sustain her joy. The home was definitely ready to experience more joy!

Step 15: Go to the Next Room and Repeat All Steps from 1 to 14

For any small spaces such as powder rooms, walk-in closets, or mudrooms, or under the stairs closet, etc., you can ask your pendulum if these spaces require an energy clearing, or you can simply use step 14 for each one to raise the level of love within that space to the highest appropriate level. If you can't easily access a room such as an attic, a basement, or a room that is full of clutter, then you can stand near the entrance and hold the image and intention within your mind of what room you are about to energetically clear.

How to Finish the Home Energy–Clearing Treatment: Four Separate Steps

Once you have finished energy clearing all the rooms within the home, there are four final steps that will help you complete the house energy-clearing treatment. The last step is for you to remeasure the overall energy of the home.

Step 1: Clear the Adverse Energetic Effects of the Surrounding Area, Neighborhood, and the Community upon the House and All of Its Inhabitants

This step simply helps clear any external energy problems that may be causing a disturbance with the property's overall vibration.

Step 2: Clear, Bless, and Empower the Auric Field of the Home

This step clears any interference or congestion within the property's main auric field. Blessing the property will also empower the protective energy field surrounding the property so that it can deflect any potential harm.

Step 3: Remeasure the Overall Energy of the Home

Now that you've successfully completed a house energy-clearing treatment, you can go ahead and remeasure the overall energy of the home to check if it's increased in vibrational resonance. If it has, then great news—just keep a check on it every month or so, and in the meantime, you can always do step 14; raise the level of love with the home to the highest appropriate level for the greatest good of all concerned. If there is no elevated change in the overall vibration when you remeasure, then you need to give it more time, because while energetic shifts take place immediately on a spiritual level, they often take more time to process, and therefore results can emerge and keep improving over a period of twenty-four hours and beyond. Energy may even continue to clear and process for several days and even weeks later, since energy clears in layers. When you leave it for twenty-four hours and then remeasure the overall energy of the home on the measurement chart, you may then notice a significant improvement. It is very rare that there will be no improvement, and if this is the case, then you may need to seek further expertise. Also, when you remeasure it will never give you a lower measurement than the one you initially took when starting. If this is the case, then you need to continue practicing and honing your dowsing skills. Why? Because by you applying the energy-clearing prayer commands, including raising the love energy within your home, you will absolutely cause a beneficial shift to take place. This will never aid in lowering the overall energy vibration of the home. The good news is that if you have completed all or most of the steps in the house energy-clearing protocol, then you will most certainly notice energetic improvements even if they do take time. The tangible results of the elevated energy now resonating within the home environment can produce wonderful benefits that can be observed and experienced over time. These include living in a more harmonious environment, connecting more deeply with family members, a feeling of inner peace within the home, and greater creativity and productivity due to the vibrational support of the home on each family member's consciousness. In this sense, external factors such as career, work, study, finances, opportunities, and auspicious relationships with others all are enhanced.

Step 4: People and Pets: Raise the Level of Love Energy

By raising the level of love energy within all people and pets who live in the home environment, you will help harmonize their energies with the new elevated energy frequencies resonating within the home. This serves and benefits the energy both of the home environment and the people and pets who live there, since higher vibrational energies all around will help sustain and maintain the positive results and outcome of the house energy-clearing treatment.

Closing and Grounding Prayer

Just as you prayed to begin the house energy-clearing treatment, so do you pray to end it. In this sense you help to detach your energy from the home environment and to ground and rebalance your own energetic equilibrium. It is also a way to offer thanksgiving to your universal support system.

Now that you've read through each step, you are ready to begin the house energy-clearing protocol.

House Energy–Clearing Protocol

Step 1: Energetic Protection and Connection Prayer (Cocreation)

The first prayer is for when you clear the energy of your own home, and the second prayer is for when you clear the energy of a loved one's or friend's home.

I ask for divine light protection within and around myself and my home as I begin a house energy-clearing treatment. I ask for divine light support to assist me in every aspect of this house energy-clearing treatment, in harmony with my greatest and highest good and the greatest and highest good of my family, my pets, the property, and all concerned. Thank you. Amen. It is done!

I ask for divine light protection within and around myself and [state name of loved one's / friend's] home as I begin a house energy-clearing treatment. I ask for divine light support to assist me in every aspect of this house energy-clearing treatment, in harmony with my greatest and highest good and the greatest and highest good of [state loved one's / friend's name], his/her family, any pets, the property, and all concerned. Thank you. Amen. It is done!

To help empower the prayer request, you can also visualize vibrant white or golden light resonating within and around you. Remember you can adapt these prayers to suit your own creative style and belief system, while also making sure that you still cover asking for energetic protection and spiritual support. Always express gratitude, which greatly amplifies the prayer request.

That's you linked in, switched on, and ready to go!

Step 2: Energy Test to Check If You Can Begin

With the pendulum in hand, ask aloud if it is appropriate to proceed with an energy-clearing treatment for "this house." If you want to say the full address of the home, then this is fine, since it is a great way to focus the mind, yet since you are standing in the home and not actually doing a distance energy-clearing treatment, then just saying "this house" is sufficient.

Step 3: Measure the Overall Energy of the Home

Use the energy measurement chart with your pendulum and ask to be shown the overall energy of the home. Take note of the measurement.

Step 4: Choose a Room to Begin and Discern Potential Energy Problems

Take any notes you want so that you can go back to the space at a later date to make the necessary physical adjustments and corrections.

Step 5: Clear the Etheric Energy of the Room

With your pendulum in hand, state the following energy-clearing command: "Clear the etheric energy pattern within this room." Your pendulum will start moving in a counterclockwise direction as it clears any energetic issues that do not support the etheric energy pattern of the room. Once your pendulum has finished moving, then you are ready for the next step.

Step 6: Clear the Emotional Energy of the Room

With your pendulum in hand, state the following energy-clearing command: "Clear any imbalanced emotional residue within this room." Your pendulum will start moving in a counterclockwise direction as it removes any congested emotional energy charges that do not support the overall energetic atmosphere of the room. Once your pendulum has finished moving, then you are ready for the next step.

Step 7: Clear the Mental Energy of the Room

With your pendulum in hand, state the following energy-clearing command: "Clear any imbalanced mental residue, and any negative thought forms and images within this room." Your pendulum will start moving in a counterclockwise direction as it removes any congested mental energy charges that include thought forms, and mental images that do not support the overall energetic atmosphere of the room. Once your pendulum has finished moving, then you are ready for the next step.

Step 8: Clear the Spiritual Energies of the Room
(Astral, Etheric Template, Celestial, and Causal)

With your pendulum in hand, state the following energy-clearing command: "Clear any nonbeneficial astral and spiritual energies within this room." This covers all four of the property's spiritual energy fields. Your pendulum will start moving in a counterclockwise direction as it removes any nonbeneficial astral and spiritual energies that do not support the overall energetic atmosphere of the room. Once your pendulum has finished moving, then you are ready for the next step.

Step 9: Clear Any Objects and Items of Furniture

Use the following energy-clearing command whether you are clearing one selected object or item of furniture or whether you are clearing them as a group: "Clear the adverse effects of any and all forms of nonbeneficial energy and interference within or attached to any object or item of furniture within this room, originating from all timelines and dimensions of experience." If you are clearing one selected item, you simply state, "within or attached to this desk" or "within or attached to this painting." Once your pendulum has finished moving, then you are ready for the next step.

Step 10: Ask If There Is Any Geopathic Stress
Adversely Affecting the Room

With your pendulum in hand, ask if there is any geopathic stress adversely affecting this room. If you receive a yes response, then use the following energy-clearing command: "Clear the adverse energetic effects of any geopathic stress interfering with this room, any family members, and pets." Your pendulum will start moving in a counterclockwise direction as it clears the adverse energetic effects of geopathic stress upon the room and upon any people and pets. Once your pendulum has finished moving, then you are ready for the next step.

Step 11: Ask If There Is Any Technological Stress
Adversely Affecting the Room

With your pendulum in hand, ask if there is any technological stress adversely affecting this room. If you receive a yes response, then use the following energy-clearing command: "Clear the adverse energetic effects of any technological stress interfering with this room, any family members, and pets." Your pendulum will start moving in a counterclockwise direction as it clears the adverse energetic effects of technological stress upon the room and upon any people and pets. Once your pendulum has finished moving, then you are ready for the next step.

Step 12: Ask If There Are Any Ghost or Spirit Energies in the Room

With your pendulum in hand, ask if there are any ghost or spirit energies in the room. If you receive a yes response, then go ahead and use the following energy-clearing command: "Clear any and all ghost residue or spirit energies within this room. Release and guide any spirits to the Spirit Realm in order that they may continue on with their soul journey, evolution, and development in the highest and best way for the good of all." Your pendulum will start moving in a counterclockwise direction as it clears any ghostly residue and spirit energy within the room. Once your pendulum has finished moving, then you are ready for the next step.

Step 13: Ask If There Are Any Energy Patterns Adversely Affecting the Room

With your pendulum in hand, ask if there are any negative energy patterns adversely affecting the room. If you receive a yes response, then go ahead and use the following energy-clearing command: "Clear any and all negative energy patterns adversely affecting this room at their point of origin." Your pendulum will start moving in a counterclockwise direction as it clears the adverse energetic effects of negative energy patterns held within the room. Once your pendulum has finished moving, then you are ready for the next step.

Step 14: Raise the Level of Love Energy in the Room to the Highest Appropriate Level

With your pendulum in hand, use the following energy-command: "Raise the level of love energy within this room to the highest appropriate level for the greatest good of all concerned." This time your pendulum will start moving in a clockwise direction as it helps elevate the frequencies of love energy within the room. Once your pendulum has finished moving, then you are ready for the next step.

Step 15: Go to the Next Room and Repeat All Steps from 1 to 14

How to Finish the Home Energy–Clearing Treatment: Four Separate Steps

Step 1: Clear the Adverse Energetic Effects of the Surrounding Area, Neighborhood, and the Community upon the House and All of Its Inhabitants

With your pendulum in hand, state the following energy-clearing command: "Clear the adverse energetic effects of the surrounding area, neighborhood, and community upon this home, all family members, and pets." The pendulum will begin to move in a counterclockwise direction as it clears the external nonbeneficial energies. Once your pendulum has finished moving, then you are ready for the next step.

Step 2: Clear, Bless, and Empower the Auric Field of the Home

With your pendulum in hand, state the following energy-clearing command: "Clear the home's auric field of all forms of nonbeneficial energies, nonbeneficial frequencies, interference, and harm." The pendulum will begin to move in a counterclockwise direction as it clears the nonbeneficial energies. Then state the following blessing: "Bless this home with a shield of divine light protection, happiness, and abundance for all who abide there." This time the pendulum will begin to move in a clockwise direction. Once your pendulum has finished moving, then you are ready for the third step.

Step 3: Remeasure the Overall Energy of the Home

Remeasure the overall energy of the home to check if it's increased in vibrational resonance. Take a note to compare it with the first measurement.

Step 4: People and Pets: Raise the Level of Love Energy

Now that you have successfully completed the house energy-clearing treatment, you can use the following energy-clearing command to raise the level of love energy within the people and pets who live in the home: "Raise the level of love energy within all people and pets in this home to the highest appropriate level in accordance with their greatest and highest good." The pendulum will begin to move in a clockwise direction. You can also do this as a separate energy-clearing command per person and pet. Example: "Raise the level of love energy within [state full name] to the highest appropriate level for his/her greatest and highest good." The pendulum will begin to move in a clockwise direction. Once your pendulum has finished moving, then you are ready for the closing and grounding prayer. If you feel that any person or pet within the household could benefit further from a personal energy-clearing treatment, then please refer to chapter 11 for the exact steps and protocol. This can be done the following day unless you want to carry on with the energy-clearing work that same day.

Closing and Grounding Prayer

You always end with a prayer of thanksgiving for the universal support and guidance. The closing and grounding prayer will also help you spiritually and energetically detach from the long-distance house energy-clearing treatment. The following prayer is an example of what you can use: "Thank you to my divine light team (or to my universal support system) for helping me with this energy-clearing treatment today. Please clear and ground my energy in the highest and best way. I now detach. Thank you. Amen. It is done!"

Well done—you've just completed an amazing house energy-clearing treatment!

CHAPTER 9

DISTANCE HOUSE ENERGY– CLEARING TREATMENT

With realization of one's own potential and self confidence in one's ability, one can build a better world.

—DALAI LAMA

A distance house energy-clearing treatment is a wonderful way of helping a loved one or friend who's located anywhere within the world, all from the comfort of your own home. You can even do a distance house energy-clearing treatment for your own home. This chapter will guide you through the exact steps and process of two different kinds of distance house energy-clearing treatments. The first one is longer since it involves working distantly on each individual room, just like the house energy-clearing treatment from the previous chapter. The second one is a much-faster process because you will be doing a distance house energy-clearing treatment on the home as one entire unit.

You will need to use the full address of the property whenever you do a distance house energy-clearing treatment, because every home address has its own specific energetic frequency and spiritual coordinates. You can think of this in the same way as when a healer sends distance spiritual healing to a person or animal, and they use their name or a visual image (or both) to identify them. Stating the full address enables you to connect with the correct property on a spiritual and energetic level, since it helps you zone directly into the etheric pattern and overall vibrational frequency of the house. Stating the full property address also helps you focus your creative visual intent on the energy of the home. Remember to do someone else's distance house energy-clearing treatment only if you have gained permission from them to do so. This is because you must respect other people's energetic environments, including the energies of all the people who live there. You can certainly offer someone you know a distance house energy-clearing treatment, and they may also request one from you, yet you don't just decide to go ahead and clear someone's home environment just because you think it's a great idea to do so. You may eventually get so good at clearing the energy in people's homes, while also being passionate about doing so, that word of mouth spreads and you begin to get requests to help others. This is also a sign that you are expanding your creative potential and responsibility to help others in this way, and so the universe will guide situations and people toward you. In the meantime, you always start with the energy of your own home environment and those of your loved ones and friends as a way of initiation into the life-changing power of distance energy clearing.

Distance House Energy–Clearing Treatment

Engaging in the process of a distance house energy-clearing treatment is a wonderful way of helping clear a loved one's or friend's home and even your own home without needing to walk through the entire property. When doing a distance house energy-clearing treatment for someone else's home, you will need to find out the following information in order to begin:

Full address: This is so you have the exact spiritual coordinates for when you cocreate the distance house energy-clearing treatment with your universal support system.

What kind of property is it? Example: condo, family home, apartment. This will help you visualize and understand what kind of property you are working with, since it helps the mind focus. How many rooms are there within the home, including the attic space and basement? This will give you an idea of how big the project is, because more rooms will take you extra time. You can then decide if you want to do protocol 1 or protocol 2. The latter protocol is used to work on as one entire unit instead of working on each individual room, and therefore it can be more convenient to use when you don't have much time.

How many people live in the home, and what are their names and ages? This will help you understand the energetic mix of people's combined vibrational frequencies. Plus, you can offer to do a personal energy-clearing treatment for anyone who may require it, or you can simply raise the level of love energy within their mind, body, and soul to help them harmonize with the new elevated vibration resonating within the home environment due to the distance house energy-clearing treatment.

How many pets live in the home? Are they healthy? Again, you can offer to do an energy-clearing treatment for them separately if required, or you can simply raise the level of love energy within their entire system to help support and empower them.

Once you've collected the information, then you are ready to begin. The following protocol explains exactly what you need to do for a distance house energy-clearing treatment, starting with the longer version.

Distance House Energy–Clearing Protocol (Long Version)

Step 1: Energetic Protection and Connection Prayer (Cocreation)

Always begin with a prayer for energetic protection and for spiritual connection to help you connect with and direct the universal clearing/healing forces of Divine Love and Light. If you are doing a distance house energy-clearing treatment for a loved one or friend, then you simply adapt the prayer to include them and their home. The following two prayers offer you an example of what you can say. The first prayer is for when you distantly clear the energy of your own home, and the second prayer is for when you do a distance house energy-clearing treatment for a loved one's or friend's home.

> I ask for divine light protection within and around myself and my home as I begin a distance house energy-clearing treatment. I ask for divine light support to assist me in every aspect of this house energy-clearing treatment, in harmony with my greatest and highest good and the greatest and highest good of my family, my pets, the property, and all concerned. Thank you. Amen. It is done!

> I ask for divine light protection within and around myself, [state name of loved one / friend] and his/her home as I begin a distance house energy-clearing treatment. I ask for divine light support to assist me in every aspect of this house energy-clearing treatment, in harmony with my greatest and highest good and the greatest and highest good of [state name of loved one / friend], his/her family, any pets, the property, and all concerned. Thank you. Amen. It is done!

To help empower the prayer request, you can also visualize vibrant white or golden light resonating within and around you. Remember you can adapt these prayers to suit your own creative style and belief system, while also making sure that you still cover asking for energetic protection and spiritual support. Always express gratitude, which greatly amplifies the prayer request.

That's you linked in, switched on, and ready to go!

Step 2: Energy Test to Check If You Can Begin

With the pendulum in hand, ask aloud if it is appropriate to proceed with a distance energy-clearing treatment for "state the full address." If the pendulum swings back and forth in the yes position, then you will know that it is appropriate to proceed. If the pendulum swings side to side in the no position, then the answer is no, and it's not appropriate to proceed at this time, so don't do it.

Step 3: Measure the Overall Energy of the Home

Use the energy measurement chart with your pendulum and ask to be shown the overall energy of the home. Take a note of the measurement.

Step 4: Choose a Room to Begin and Discern Potential Energy Problems

This time you are energetically connecting to the room without physically seeing it, and so you must rely on your intuition to obtain information. You can use a notebook to jot down information that you want to remember later, so that you can talk about any impressions you picked up with your friend or loved one or to remember what you sensed within your own home. It really doesn't matter if you don't receive any impressions at all; you just move on to the next step. This step, however, is typically one that can help you fine-tune your intuitive nature.

Ask yourself the following questions to help activate your intuition: If the room could speak to you, what personality and character does it have? Does it emanate joy, sadness, loneliness, fear, etc.? Does the overall energy of the room feel busy, noisy, chaotic, quiet, still, or even lifeless?

Do you clairvoyantly observe any areas of clutter, any dark spaces, or anything broken, leaking, or in need of general repair? If so, these are aspects of the room that need to be physically adjusted in order to help support the overall energetic balance of that particular space. Take notes of any and all impressions you get. Sometimes you will be amazed at the feedback you receive when discussing your impressions. Don't place any pressure on yourself to receive any information, since this simply blocks the flow of your intuition. Sometimes you will receive plenty of impressions, and other times hardly any or none. It's not important; it's only a step to help you get acquainted with different kinds of energetic information.

Are you intuitively sensing any colors within the room? Noticing things like this can help you make decisions about making specific changes to the color of the room, or for offering beneficial suggestions to a friend or loved one.

Now that you've discerned the overall energy of the room and you've taken notes of any intuitive impressions, you will have gained valuable insight into what needs to be addressed within this particular space. You can discuss with your friend or loved one the necessary adjustments and corrections that can help improve the overall energy and atmosphere of the space.

It's now time to begin the next step and your first energy-clearing command!

Step 5: Clear the Etheric Energy of the Room

With your pendulum in hand, state the following energy-clearing command: "Clear the etheric energy pattern within this room." Your pendulum will start moving in a counterclockwise direction as it clears any energetic issues that do not support the etheric energy pattern of the room. Once your pendulum has finished moving, then you are ready for the next step.

Step 6: Clear the Emotional Energy of the Room

With your pendulum in hand, state the following energy-clearing command: "Clear any imbalanced emotional residue within this room." Your pendulum will start moving in a counterclockwise direction as it removes any congested emotional-energy charges that do not support the overall energetic atmosphere of the room. Once your pendulum has finished moving, then you are ready for the next step.

Step 7: Clear the Mental Energy of the Room

With your pendulum in hand, state the following energy-clearing command: "Clear any imbalanced mental residue, negative thought forms, and images within this room." Your pendulum will start moving in a counterclockwise direction as it removes any congested mental energy charges that include thought forms and mental images that do not support the overall energetic atmosphere of the room. Once your pendulum has finished moving, then you are ready for the next step.

Step 8: Clear the Spiritual Energies of the Room

With your pendulum in hand, state the following energy-clearing command: "Clear any nonbeneficial astral and spiritual energies within this room." This covers all four of the property's spiritual energy fields. The first of the four spiritual fields is associated with the heart and soul energy of the body, since it holds the energy frequencies of unconditional love, inner peace, and harmony. Your pendulum will start moving in a counterclockwise direction as it removes any nonbeneficial astral and spiritual energies that do not support the overall energetic atmosphere of the room. Once your pendulum has finished moving, then you are ready for the next step.

Step 9: Clear Any Objects and Items of Furniture

When doing a distance home energy-clearing treatment, you will be clearing the energy of any objects or items of furniture within the room in one go and not separately. Use the following energy-clearing command: "Clear the adverse effects of any and all forms of nonbeneficial energy and interference within or attached to any object or item of furniture within this room, originating from all timelines and dimensions of experience." Once your pendulum has finished moving, then you are ready for the next step.

Step 10: Ask If There Is Any Geopathic Stress Adversely Affecting the Room

With your pendulum in hand, ask if there is any geopathic stress adversely affecting this room. If you receive a yes response, then use the following energy-clearing command: "Clear the adverse energetic effects of any geopathic stress interfering with this room, any family members, and pets." Your pendulum will start moving in a counterclockwise direction as it clears the adverse energetic effects of geopathic stress upon the room and upon any people and pets. Once your pendulum has finished moving, then you are ready for the next step.

Step 11: Ask If There Is Any Technological Stress Adversely Affecting the Room

With your pendulum in hand, ask if there is any technological stress adversely affecting this room. If you receive a yes response, then use the following energy-clearing command: "Clear the adverse energetic effects of any technological stress interfering with this room, any family members, and pets." Your pendulum will start moving in a counterclockwise direction as it clears the adverse energetic effects of technological stress upon the room and upon any people and pets. Once your pendulum has finished moving, then you are ready for the next step.

Step 12: Ask If There Are Any Ghost or Spirit Energies in the Room

With your pendulum in hand, ask if there are any ghost or spirit energies in the room. If you receive a yes response, then go ahead and use the following energy-clearing command: "Clear any and all ghost residue or spirit energies within this room. Release and guide any spirits to the Spirit Realm in order that they may continue on with their soul journey, evolution, and development in the highest and best way for the good of all." Your pendulum will start moving in a counterclockwise direction as it clears any ghostly residue and spirit energy within the room. Once your pendulum has finished moving, then you are ready for the next step.

Step 13: Ask If There Are Any Energy Patterns Adversely Affecting the Room

With your pendulum in hand, ask if there are any negative energy patterns adversely affecting the room. If you receive a yes response, then go ahead and use the following energy-clearing command: "Clear any and all negative energy patterns adversely affecting this room at their point of origin." Your pendulum will start moving in a counterclockwise direction as it clears the adverse energetic effects of negative energy patterns held within the room. Once your pendulum has finished moving, then you are ready for the next step.

Step 14: Raise the Level of Love Energy in the Room to the Highest Appropriate Level

With your pendulum in hand, use the following energy-healing command: "Raise the level of love energy within this room to the highest appropriate level for the greatest good of all concerned." This time your pendulum will start moving in a clockwise direction as it helps elevate the frequencies of love energy within the room. Once your pendulum has finished moving, then you are ready for the next step.

Step 15: Go to the Next Room and Repeat All Steps from 1 to 14.

How to Finish the Distance House–Energy Clearing Treatment: Four Separate Steps

Step 1: Clear the Adverse Energetic Effects of the Surrounding Area, Neighborhood, and the Community upon the House and All of Its Inhabitants

With your pendulum in hand, state the following energy-clearing command: "Clear the adverse energetic effects of the surrounding area, neighborhood, and community upon this home, all family members, and pets." The pendulum will begin to move in a counterclockwise direction as it clears the nonbeneficial energies. Once your pendulum has finished moving, then you are ready for the next step.

Step 2: Clear, Bless, and Empower the Auric Field of the Home

With your pendulum in hand, state the following energy-clearing command: "Clear the home's auric field of all forms of nonbeneficial energies, nonbeneficial frequencies, interference, and harm." The pendulum will begin to move in a counterclockwise direction as it clears the nonbeneficial energies. Then state the following blessing: "Bless this home with a shield of divine light protection, happiness, and abundance for all who abide there." This time the pendulum will begin to move in a clockwise direction. Once your pendulum has finished moving, then you are ready for the third step.

Step 3: Remeasure the Overall Energy of the Home

Remeasure the overall energy of the home to check if it has increased in vibrational resonance. Take a note to compare it with the first measurement.

Step 4: People and Pets: Raise the Level of Love Energy

Now that you have successfully completed the distance house energy-clearing treatment, you can use the following energy-healing command to raise the level of love energy within the people and pets who live in the home. "Raise the level of love energy within all people and pets in this home to the highest appropriate level in accordance with their greatest and highest good." The pendulum will begin to move in a clockwise direction. You can also do this as a separate energy-clearing command per person and pet. Example: "Raise the level of love energy within [state full name] to the highest appropriate level for his/her greatest and highest good." The pendulum will begin to move in a clockwise direction. Once your pendulum has finished moving, then you are ready for the closing and grounding prayer. If you feel that any person or pet within the household could benefit further from a personal energy-clearing treatment, then please refer to chapter 11 for the exact steps and protocol. This can be done the following day unless you want to carry on with the energy-clearing work that same day.

Closing and Grounding Prayer

You always end with a prayer of thanksgiving for the universal support and guidance. The closing and grounding prayer will also help you spiritually and energetically detach from the distance house energy-clearing treatment. The following prayer is an example of what you can use. "Thank you to my divine light team (or to my universal support system) for helping me with this energy-clearing treatment today. Please clear and ground my energy in the highest and best way. I now detach. Thank you. Amen. It is done!"

Well done—you've just completed an amazing distance house energy-clearing treatment!

Next you will find out how to do a shorter version of a distance house energy-clearing treatment.

Distance House Energy–Clearing Protocol (Short Version)

You can use this shortened distance house energy-clearing protocol for when you don't have much time to spare. The way that it's shortened is that you will energy-clear the home as one environment and not have to go through each and every room individually. Plus, you don't need to spend time discerning the potential energy problems of the home in step 4 unless you really want to. While you will still receive very beneficial results with this shortened protocol, the longer one can offer a more in-depth energy-clearing treatment that can at times produce greater results.

Step 1: Energetic Protection and Connection Prayer (Cocreation)

The following two prayers offer you an example of what you can say. The first prayer is for when you distantly clear the energy of your own home, and the second prayer is for when you do a distance house energy-clearing treatment for a loved one's or friend's home.

I ask for divine light protection within and around myself and my home as I begin a distance house energy-clearing treatment. I ask for divine light support to assist me in every aspect of this house energy-clearing treatment, in harmony with my greatest and highest good and the greatest and highest good of my family, my pets, the property, and all concerned. Thank you. Amen. It is done!

I ask for divine light protection within and around myself and [state name of loved one's / friend's] home as I begin a distance house energy-clearing treatment. I ask for divine light support to assist me in every aspect of this house energy-clearing treatment, in harmony with my greatest and highest good and the greatest and highest good of [state loved one's / friend's name], his/her family, any pets, the property, and all concerned. Thank you. Amen. It is done!

To help empower the prayer request, you can also visualize vibrant white or golden light resonating within and around you. Remember you can adapt these prayers to suit your own creative style and belief system, while also making sure that you still cover asking for energetic protection and spiritual support. Always express gratitude, which greatly amplifies the prayer request.

That's you linked in, switched on, and ready to go!

Step 2: Energy Test to Check If You Can Begin

With the pendulum in hand, ask aloud if it is appropriate to proceed with a distance energy-clearing treatment for "state full address." If the pendulum swings back and forth in the yes position, then you will know that it is appropriate to proceed. If the pendulum swings side to side in the no position, then the answer is no, and it's not appropriate to proceed at this time, so don't do it.

Step 3: Measure the Overall Energy of the Home

Use the energy measurement chart with your pendulum and ask to be shown the overall energy of the home. Take a note of the measurement.

Step 4: Discern Potential Energy Problems

You can do this step if you want to by intuitively discerning the overall energy of the home environment. If not, just move on to the next step.

Step 5: Clear the Etheric Energy of the House

With your pendulum in hand, state the following energy-clearing command: "Clear the etheric energy pattern within this house." Your pendulum will start moving in a counterclockwise direction as it clears any energetic issues that do not support the etheric energy pattern of the house. Once your pendulum has finished moving, then you are ready for the next step.

Step 6: Clear the Emotional Energy of the House

With your pendulum in hand, state the following energy-clearing command: "Clear any imbalanced emotional residue within this house." Your pendulum will start moving in a counterclockwise direction as it removes any congested emotional-energy charges that do not support the overall energetic atmosphere of the house. Once your pendulum has finished moving, then you are ready for the next step.

Step 7: Clear the Mental Energy of the House

With your pendulum in hand, state the following energy-clearing command: "Clear any imbalanced mental residue and negative thought forms and images within this house." Your pendulum will start moving in a counterclockwise direction as it removes any congested mental energy charges that include thought forms and mental images that do not support the overall energetic atmosphere of the house. Once your pendulum has finished moving, then you are ready for the next step.

Step 8: Clear the Spiritual Energies of the House

With your pendulum in hand, state the following energy-clearing command: "Clear any nonbeneficial astral and spiritual energies within this house." This covers all four of the property's spiritual energy fields. Your pendulum will start moving in a counterclockwise direction as it removes any nonbeneficial astral and spiritual energies that do not support the overall energetic atmosphere of the house. Once your pendulum has finished moving, then you are ready for the next step.

Step 9: Clear Any Objects and Items of Furniture

When doing a distance home energy-clearing treatment, you will be clearing the energy of any objects or items of furniture within the home in one go and not separately. Use the following energy-clearing command: "Clear the adverse effects of any and all forms of nonbeneficial energy and interference within or attached to any object or item of furniture within this house, originating from all timelines and dimensions of experience." Once your pendulum has finished moving, then you are ready for the next step.

Step 10: Ask If There Is Any Geopathic Stress Adversely Affecting the House

With your pendulum in hand, ask if there is any geopathic stress adversely affecting this house. If you receive a yes response, then use the following energy-clearing command: "Clear the adverse energetic effects of any geopathic stress interfering with this house, any family members, and pets." Your pendulum will start moving in a counterclockwise direction as it clears the adverse energetic effects of geopathic stress upon the home and upon any people and pets. Once your pendulum has finished moving, then you are ready for the next step.

Step 11: Ask If There Is Any Technological Stress Adversely Affecting the House

With your pendulum in hand, ask if there is any technological stress adversely affecting this house. If you receive a yes response, then use the following energy-clearing command: "Clear the adverse energetic effects of any technological stress interfering with this house, any family members, and pets." Your pendulum will start moving in a counterclockwise direction as it clears the adverse energetic effects of technological stress upon the home and upon any people and pets. Once your pendulum has finished moving, then you are ready for the next step.

Step 12: Ask If There Are Any Ghost or Spirit Energies in the House

With your pendulum in hand, ask if there are any ghost or spirit energies in the house. If you receive a yes response, then go ahead and use the following energy-clearing command: "Clear any and all ghost residue or spirit energies within this house. Release and guide any spirits to the Spirit Realm in order that they may continue on with their soul journey, evolution, and development in the highest and best way for the good of all." Your pendulum will start moving in a counterclockwise direction as it clears any ghostly residue and spirit energy within the house. Once your pendulum has finished moving, then you are ready for the next step.

Step 13: Ask If There Are Any Energy Patterns
Adversely Affecting the House

With your pendulum in hand, ask if there are any negative energy patterns adversely affecting the house. If you receive a yes response, then go ahead and use the following energy-clearing command: "Clear any and all negative energy patterns adversely affecting this house at their point of origin." Your pendulum will start moving in a counterclockwise direction as it clears the adverse energetic effects of negative energy patterns held within the home. Once your pendulum has finished moving, then you are ready for the next step.

Step 14: Raise the Level of Love Energy in the House to
the Highest Appropriate Level

With your pendulum in hand, use the following energy-healing command: "Raise the level of love energy within this home to the highest appropriate level for the greatest good of all concerned." This time your pendulum will start moving in a clockwise direction as it helps elevate the frequencies of love energy within the home. Once your pendulum has finished moving, then you are ready for the next step.

How to Finish the Distance House Energy–Clearing Treatment: Three Separate Steps

Step 1: Clear the Adverse Energetic Effects of the Surrounding Area,
Neighborhood, and the Community upon the House and
All of Its Inhabitants

With your pendulum in hand, state the following energy-clearing command: "Clear the adverse energetic effects of the surrounding area, neighborhood, and community upon this home, all family members, and pets." The pendulum will begin to move in a counterclockwise direction as it clears the nonbeneficial energies. Once your pendulum has finished moving, then you are ready for the next step.

Step 2: Clear, Bless, and Empower the Auric Field of the Home

With your pendulum in hand, state the following energy-clearing command: "Clear the home's auric field of all forms of nonbeneficial energies, nonbeneficial frequencies, interference, and harm." The pendulum will begin to move in a counterclockwise direction as it clears the nonbeneficial energies. Then state the following blessing: "Bless this home with a shield of divine light protection, happiness, and abundance for all who abide there." This time the pendulum will begin to move in a clockwise direction. Once your pendulum has finished moving, then you are ready for the third step.

Step 3: Remeasure the Overall Energy of the Home

Remeasure the overall energy of the home to check if it increased in vibrational resonance. Take a note to compare it with the first measurement.

Step 4: People and Pets: Raise the Level of Love Energy

Now that you have successfully completed the distance house energy-clearing treatment, you can use the following energy-healing command to raise the level of love energy within the people and pets who live in the home. "Raise the level of love energy within all people and pets in this home to the highest appropriate level in accordance with their greatest and highest good." The pendulum will begin to move in a clockwise direction. You can also do this as a separate energy-clearing command per person and pet. Example: "Raise the level of love energy within [state full name] to the highest appropriate level for his/her greatest and highest good." The pendulum will begin to move in a clockwise direction. Once your pendulum has finished moving, then you are ready for the closing and grounding prayer. If you feel that any person or pet within the household could benefit further from a personal energy-clearing treatment, then please refer to chapter 11 for the exact steps and protocol. This can be done the following day unless you want to carry on with the energy-clearing work that same day.

Closing and Grounding Prayer

The following prayer is an example of what you can use. "Thank you to my divine light team (or to my universal support system) for helping me with this energy-clearing treatment today. Please clear and ground my energy in the highest and best way. I now detach. Thank you. Amen. It is done!"

Well done—you've just completed an amazing distance house energy-clearing treatment!

CHAPTER 10

BUSINESS ENERGY-CLEARING TREATMENT

Success is not the key to happiness. Happiness is the key to success.
If you love what you are doing, you will be successful.

—Albert Schweitzer

An energy-clearing treatment of a business premises and of the actual business itself can help turn current and potential problems around and will support the overall business concept and plan. Stress, anxiety, and business pressures involving financial struggle, wages, rent, staff, customers, and clients, among other business-related issues, can energetically overwhelm the entire business enterprise. This creates a chaotic frequency that can interfere with the optimal flow and function of the business. A chaotic frequency can become a hotbed for attracting further problems—as the saying goes, "Misery loves company." In this sense, the stress factor is responsible for the business creating and attracting further problems or in continuously persisting with the ones it has. While there will always be the occasional hiccups in business and in life, since nothing is ever really guaranteed, if there are continuous problems with the success of a business, then there can be several different energetic factors and forces that interplay to interfere with, cause, and contribute to them. A business energy-clearing treatment will help address these issues so that the potential success of the business has more freedom to succeed.

Every individual business has two main energy patterns associated with it that can help support and generate potential success for the business. The first energy pattern is the collective one, regarding a specific business genre and theme. For instance, the collective energy pattern of all hair salons will be different from the collective energy pattern of all bakeries or of all fashion boutiques or of all chartered accountants or of all law firms, etc. This unique energy pattern is equivalent to an energetic map for the new business to travel through and expand into, which at its most optimal destination can be super successful. Why? Because there are very successful businesses in your specific niche who have already journeyed their way into that optimal outcome, and if they can do it, so can you. The only way where this preordained energetic map would not be so is if you are the inventor of something completely new that no one else on planet Earth has previously thought of. In this case, you would be the instigator of a brand-new energy pattern that will have unlimited potential for creative expansion—yet, nothing is guaranteed because it is the first of its kind. Teething problems and early setbacks of a new invention can also be the beginning of something that can evolve into global success, and so time, patience, and dedication will be required. People often give up way too soon because they are looking for instantaneous success, yet any setbacks can simply be to help the product or service become more refined and to take greater shape and make it ready for its breakthrough. Take Thomas Edison, for instance, an American inventor and businessman who is said to hold over one thousand US patents in his name, as well as having patents in other countries. This man used the power of his creative intelligence to bring into reality new ideas that could benefit humanity. You have this same unlimited and untapped creative intelligence within you that is unique to you.

The collective energy pattern of a specific business niche is strengthened by every new business of that same niche that comes along. The collective energy pattern of a business will also continue evolving as humanity evolves, and especially when humanity benefits from the product or service in some way. If and when this energy pattern is no longer required as humanity evolves along the ages, then it will either adapt and evolve into something else or the energy will be transformed back to universal intelligence ready for ever-new creations. Everything within our universe is always in the process of creative motion and expansion, and nothing is ever really destroyed; it is simply transformed.

Many small business ventures often fail to get off the ground before they have a chance to begin the journey of their specific energy map. There are many reasons for this, both personal and business related, yet if they pick themselves up, dust themselves off, and begin again, then success is always still a possibility and probability for them, because we must remember that the energy pattern of their specific business niche has already reached that point of growth and creative expansion. The energy map will have collectively overcome many of the pitfalls within that niche, so that others within that same niche that follow along after will have a greater chance of succeeding. The collective minds of all those taking part in a specific business niche will continue to evolve the energy pattern and map together to serve future generations. Often, patience, time, and perseverance are the qualities required as one navigates the energy map that can lead them toward a probable successful outcome.

The collective energy pattern of a business niche can also be thought of as the primary soul of the business, whereas your own business will have its own soul energy that can be supported by the primary one. Everything within the universe has a soul or energy pattern. Our soul is the energy pattern of our body and consciousness. Our Spirit is the energy pattern of divinity, Creation, Light, and Absolute Love. *New York Times* bestselling author Dr. and Master Zhi Gang Sha[16] says the following about the soul:

> Soul is the boss. A human being's soul is the boss of the human being. An animal's soul is the boss of the animal. An organization's soul is the boss of the organization. A city's soul is the boss of the city.

The second energy pattern associated with a business is much more personalized and takes into account the skills, wisdom, knowledge, talents, character, and personality of the business owner, along with their personal karma. These all combine together to create the energetic ingredients that interplay with the collective energy pattern of the business. Both energy patterns work in harmony with one another to help the business blossom and grow. Our character and personality are refined and strengthened through gaining a variety of different life experiences until we find that we have a greater understanding and awareness of how we can address and respond to life challenges and problems from a higher spiritual perspective. This is what helps develop our innate wisdom so that our life challenges become less stressful and even less frequent. Any kind of so-called failure is therefore nothing more than a detour to help guide us along another path, or if we do happen to venture back along the same path, then it can help us tweak the way we do things along that path until it eventually produces different results. More-satisfying ones!

Are you doing what you are being intuitively called to do, or are you settling for something else? What about the talents and knowledge you need for your specific business? Have you taken the time to study and gain the knowledge and experience you require for your particular business niche so that you can offer the best of your own soul's light to the world? Our study, research, and experience of our business niche are important parts of our business success. We would not think of teaching others ballet dance lessons if we had never danced before, had never studied and experienced ballet, or had no personal interest in ballet whatsoever. If we did, we would surely fail with a crash, bang, and wallop as we fall to the ground. Study and research help us develop the skills and knowledge we require for potential business success. Daily practice of our emerging skill set will help us strengthen our unique talents so that we will gain the necessary experience that leads one to fulfillment, success, and service. Catherine Zeta Jones, a remarkable dancer and actress born and raised in my hometown of Swansea, South Wales, UK, aspired to be an actress from a young age. Throughout her childhood and teenage years, she was totally dedicated to her passion and purpose and was forever practicing and nurturing her natural talents with dance lessons, singing, and acting. She went on to study musical theater in London and made her stage breakthrough with a leading role in a 1987 production of *42nd Street*. After completing many successful Hollywood roles, Catherine starred in the film adaptation of the Broadway musical *Chicago* (2002), as the murderous nightclub singer Velma Kelly.[17] This is where Catherine's extraordinary talents and many years of practice and experience came pouring out into her great creative splendor. Catherine shone in that role as she gave it her all. She won an Academy Award and a Bafta, among others, yet it is plain to see that her greatest joy was in the creative expression of all that she was, which fully manifested itself within that role. Just like the quote at the top of this chapter says:

> Success is not the key to happiness. Happiness is the key to success. If you love what you are doing, you will be successful. —Albert Schweitzer

Our personal karma takes into account our financial karma and our relationship karma. Both of these aspects interplay their energy patterns in our potential business success.

Financial Karma

Financial karma involves how we deal with our interactions with money and our personal service to the world. It takes into account our financial maturity or lack of it and how wise or unwise we are with managing our income stream. We are not being punished by the universe for any lack of finances in our life. Why? Because we are 100 percent responsible for our free-will choices with money. Greed, corruption, stealing, or any kind of insincere act regarding the attainment of money is made out of one's own personal free-will choice. Unwise choices that lead a person into accumulating debt are also the result of their free will. The person's own energy vibration will resonate their interactions with money and establish an energy pattern of their overall financial relationship. As people naturally mature in their relationship with money, often due to their age and other people's positive influence, they will see a positive shift occur and money will begin to flow in. As they mature in this way, they will break free of their old energy patterns and alter their karmic relationship with money. If a person is unable to mature for reasons such as lack of wisdom and understanding of how money flows and accumulates in one's life, or due to their refusal to take responsibility for their interaction with money, or due to them acquiring money in unethical ways without them adding any sincere service to the world, then karmic rebalancing will be required as a way to help the person reharmonize their relationship with money and service. You may think that you know of one or two folks who are superrich who got their money by corrupt measures, and yet they still experience their immense wealth with no karma and therefore must have no karmic rebalancing going on in their life. This however is not true, since no one escapes from karmic rebalancing due to their own free-will decisions and actions. What you are perceiving is the space before it happens; however, it's not our business to impinge on another's karmic lessons, which can manifest as an array of life challenges, not just the financial kind.

Karmic rebalancing begins with a variety of life lessons that can take place at any time. Again, this is not a form of punishment by any external source; it is simply the outworking of a perfect harmonious universal law that enables a human being to overcome any personal challenges they have with money or to make amends for any misuse of finances. Financial lessons can therefore lead a person back toward developing greater financial flow and to be more vibrationally open to universal abundance. The universe is always supporting you even when you think you just can't catch a break. Surrendering any resistance to the life challenge you may be going through, and making amends through personal service, will certainly propel you forward in clearing up your financial karma. The truth is that you have creative dominion over your finances, health, and life opportunities, and you can begin to turn things around at any time you decide to.

Before you begin to accumulate money, you will first notice that it begins to steadily flow in and out of your life without resistance. Prior to this, money may have been sporadic as it came for a period of time and then went. As money begins to steadily flow, you begin to develop greater trust in an abundant universe to know that as you release money and as you receive money through offering sincere heartfelt service to others, then acquiring money will no longer be an issue. We all learn how to give and receive energetic exchanges not just with money but with our time, with our unconditional love, and with our personal service. Steve Chandler says the following about money:

> There are many stories and accounts about the winners of lotteries who are jubilant when they win, but whose lives descend into a nightmare after acquiring that unearned money. (No challenge, no skill.) The lottery looks like "the answer" to people because they associate money with pleasure. But the true enjoyment of money comes in part from the earning of it, which involves skill and challenge. Watching television is usually done for pleasure. That's why so few people can remember (or make use of) any of the thirty hours of television they have watched in the past week.

The good news is that we can energetically clear our overall vibration of the adverse energetic effects of any financial problems or misuse of money that we may have experienced. These energy patterns resonating within our personal energy fields limit our creative relationship with money, and once cleared we can regain more financial freedom. When we forgive others and ourselves for any prior financial hardship or misuse of money, then we regain our creative power. Forgiving leads to us choosing different thoughts, behaviors, and actions with money, which is what clears the energetic patterns and ties to our past. We often inherit our parents' belief system about money, be it supportive or limiting for us, as well as us being influenced by the culture and environment that we are born into. Being born into poverty or into a less-than-privileged environment doesn't mean that we are doomed and fated into a life of hardship and struggle. You are able to overcome anything with the creative power that permanently exists within you. Paramahansa Yogananda says the following about karma and fate:

Since all effects or seeds of our past actions, our karma, can be destroyed by roasting them in the fire of meditation, concentration, the light of the superconsciousness, and right actions. There is no such thing as fate. You make your own destiny. God has given you independence, and you are free to shut out His power, or let it in.

Our soul history also plays a part in our financial karma. Past-life experiences may still carry energy patterns regarding money that can directly influence our consciousness and our interactions and relationship with money in this life. Vows of poverty may still resonate within us that can push money away. Again, we have the ability to clear our "soul history energy," shift our consciousness toward creative freedom, and elevate our overall vibration in regard to our financial karma.

Right now, you may be on the fringe edge of financial increase as new energy patterns are processing. During this time, when you feel and observe that nothing is progressing, it is important to keep faith that things are happening in your favor behind the scenes of your life. Energy-clearing treatments are super beneficial toward speeding up this process. Why? Because you willingly use your free will and your soul's creative power to clear the layers of resistance.

Relationship Karma

Our relationship karma involves our spiritual and energetic connection that we have with others and how we generally interact with them and treat them. Do we approach them from a place of understanding, compassion, and kindness, or do we disrespect them, want to gain our personal power over them, and manipulate them? How we treat others is a measurement of how spiritually evolved we are. We all exist at different levels of spiritual maturity, and we are all continuously evolving these levels throughout our life as we clear layers of resistance toward being our authentic selves. In business, you will be dealing with many people's energies, and you will form business and personal relationships with your staff, your employees, your customers, and your clients. What kind of client or customer do you want to attract? What kind of employee do you want to have work for you? Do you offer a product or service to others that is heart centered or one that is self-centered? What kind of boss are you? Fair and supportive or dominant and unsupportive? Do you have a problem with clients paying you on time or not paying you at all? All of these answers represent your relationship karma and your energy exchanges between others.

I was asked to do an energy-clearing treatment for a business whose staff were continuously arguing with each other. Most days, complaints got back to the boss, who got totally fed up with the disharmony and infighting among his employees. I found out from the boss that the business premises had recently gone through a structural change where they had purchased the business next door and had knocked walls down to make it into one big business. New offices were now located on the first floor, and the boss moved from the top floor to the first floor. Staff members were relocated to different offices, and so they no longer shared the same dynamics with each other. Envy over who worked where and who got to work in the newer office space was causing friction, which got in the way of the business running smoothly. An energy-clearing treatment of the business premises and of the staff members, including the boss, helped restore a certain amount of harmony within the workplace. When there is a large group of staff members there will always be some discord between people. Soon the business was back on track; however, there was still one lingering problem that didn't shift. I was told that one particular staff member was always difficult from the very start, and she had worked in the business for over fifteen years. While she was excellent at her job, her personality and character loved drama, and she was always at the forefront of stirring up arguments between others or she was always complaining about the quality of other staff members' work. One energy-clearing treatment for this woman, or several, for that matter, was not going to shift the deep-seated patterns of her attitude and behavior, since this is the responsibility of her own free will to do so, and she has to truly want to personally develop, transform, and spiritually mature. If someone has no desire to improve their attitude, then energy-clearing treatments will not override their free will. Energy-clearing treatments always work in harmony with a person's greatest good, which in the staff members' case would be to help her move toward a more harmonious interaction with others, yet this is still her personal choice. Her delight in creating drama may be more important to her at this time in her life than her desire for personal growth. There is no judgment in this, since everyone is entitled to evolve their consciousness in their own time frame. In this sense, the relationship karma created between the woman and the boss will continue as it is until the boss decides any differently. At present the woman's work is of a high standard, and so the boss accepts the way she is, even though it causes excess stress within the workplace. The boss will also be learning a lesson of personal growth in the interaction with this staff member. In allowing the woman to take liberties within the workplace, the boss gives away his personal power. Setting boundaries with the woman can help the boss in this situation, yet if these boundaries are continuously broken, then the boss is going to continue in that lesson. Yet, if we look at the same situation from a higher perspective, the boss also offers unconditional love for the woman to be herself, mixed with the hope that the woman will one day wake up and become a more harmonious individual. Whom we have working for us or with us is a reflection of our own consciousness, and each karmic relationship we share with another also reveals what areas we need to work on within us to help us grow.

The good news is that your business or one that you are thinking of beginning already has unlimited potential to be successful because of the invisible collective energy pattern already set in place. Yet, not all businesses will reach their optimal potential for success. Your personal energies interact with the business in a way that makes what you do completely unique. You can think of your business as an energetic extension of your consciousness. What are your personal intentions for the business? While it's absolutely fine for you to want to be a success and to gain financial freedom, if this is your only intention and reason for the business, then you will shift off your spiritual equilibrium, which is to always use your creative force for the good of all. In this sense, when your intention also aligns with your desire to create a product or service for the good of all, where you help bring joy and benefit to others, then not only are you in harmony with your spiritual equilibrium, but you will also attract universal support to help you.

I once worked in a hair salon on a busy main street that also had another hair salon right next door. I was sixteen at the time and wondered about the competition of the two salons and whether one was better than the other. I loved the salon I was working in, yet the other one was more fashionable and attracted a younger clientele. Both salons were busy in their own unique way. Both salons had the same collective energy pattern and field supporting their business, yet their individual energetic makeup included the look and design of the business premises, the staff's personal energies, and the salon owner's specific business intention and desire. The location of both salons was very favorable, since location is also a determining factor in whether people are able to find and see a specific business; yet, with today's marketing skills and online presence, location is less a concern than it used to be. One day, I was working at the salon when there was a problem with the plumbing and the water was switched off in the salon next door. They asked us if we would be able to help by them running a pipe from our salon to theirs, since they were super booked up with clients that day, as were we. Our salon agreed and helped them out, and harmony in their salon was restored. I realized that day that there was no need for any competition between each salon, since each salon had its own unique vibe and they were both as good as each other in their own personal ways. Also, in being supportive of each other, both salons generated good karma between them. This is an important lesson because the energies of envy and greed do interfere with a person's business. If you have a business that is still growing into potential success, then the best thing that you can do is to always be happy for those who do the same work as you and who are already successful. Wish them well, wish them further success. Know that in doing so you will free the resistance along your own path toward success.

Two Distance Business Energy–Clearing Treatments

The first distance business energy-clearing treatment is formulated around clearing the energetic blockages, imbalances, and karmic energies of your unique business. The second distance energy-clearing treatment is formulated around clearing the energy of any business premises you own and work from. It can also be done in person, just like the house energy-clearing treatment, if this is what you would prefer to do. If you happen to work from home and not from a separate business premises, then you can always clear the energy of your workspace or office room.

What you are about to do is to help clear energetic resistance toward your business becoming more successful. It is a spiritual, energetic, and creative way to roll the dice in your favor. Energy clears in layers and will always work in harmony with what's best for you, because you are working with universal intelligence. Sometimes results may be slower than other times, yet you can measure these improvements by the tangible results they bring.

Distance Business Energy–Clearing Protocol

Step 1: Energetic Protection and Connection Prayer (Cocreation)

The following two prayers offer you an example of what you can say. The first prayer is for when you distantly clear the energy of your own business, and the second prayer is for when you do a distance business energy-clearing treatment for a loved one or friend.

I ask for divine light protection within and around myself and my business as I begin a distance business energy-clearing treatment. I ask for divine light support to assist me in every aspect of this energy clearing treatment, in harmony with my greatest and highest good and the greatest and highest good of my business and all concerned. Thank you. Amen. It is done!

I ask for divine light protection within and around myself, [state full name of loved one / friend], and his/her business as I begin a distance business energy-clearing treatment. I ask for divine light support to assist me in every aspect of this energy-clearing treatment, in harmony with my greatest and highest good and the greatest and highest good of [state full name of loved one / friend], his/her business, and all concerned. Thank you. Amen. It is done!

To help empower the prayer request, you can also visualize vibrant white or golden light resonating within and around you. Remember you can adapt these prayers to suit your own creative style and belief system, while also making sure that you still cover asking for energetic protection and spiritual support. Always express gratitude, which greatly amplifies the prayer request.

That's you linked in, switched on, and ready to go!

Step 2: Energy Test to Check if You Can Begin

With the pendulum in hand, ask aloud if it is appropriate to proceed with a distance business energy-clearing treatment for myself or (state full name of loved one / friend). If the pendulum swings back and forth in the yes position, then you will know that it is appropriate to proceed. If the pendulum swings side to side in the no position, then the answer is no, and it's not appropriate to proceed at this time, so don't do it.

Step 3: Measure the Overall Energy of the Business

Use the energy measurement chart with your pendulum and ask to be shown the overall energy of the business. Take a note of the measurement.

Step 4: Clear and Harmonize the Energy of the Business with the Energy of Optimal Success

With your pendulum in hand, state the following energy-healing command: "Clear any and all nonbeneficial energies and resistance that interfere with the success of my business." Your pendulum will start moving in a counterclockwise direction as it clears any interference. To harmonize the energy of your business with the energy of success, state the following: "Harmonize the energy of my business with the energy of optimal success." Your pendulum will start moving in a clockwise direction as it helps align the potential success of your business with the energy of optimal success. This energy-healing command works in harmony with the collective energy pattern that is the energy map of your business. Once your pendulum has finished moving, then you are ready for the next step.

Step 5: Clear and Harmonize Your Business Relationships

With your pendulum in hand, state the following energy-clearing command: "Clear any and all nonbeneficial energies and interference created between myself and any of my employees, staff, customers, and clients, in harmony with the greatest and highest good of my business and of all concerned." Your pendulum will start moving in a counterclockwise direction as it helps clear any negative energy that can interfere with your business and your business relationships. To harmonize with your business relationships, state the following energy-healing command. "Harmonize my business relationships with any and all employees, staff, customers, and clients in the highest and best way for my business and for all involved." This time the pendulum will start moving in a clockwise direction as it helps harmonize the collective personal energies, including your own, of all who are involved with your business in some way. Once your pendulum has finished moving, then you are ready for the next step.

Step 6: Clear and Amplify Your Financial Flow

With your pendulum in hand, state the following energy-clearing command: "Clear my financial flow from the adverse energetic effects of any and all debt energy, blockages, and imbalances." Your pendulum will start moving in a counterclockwise direction as it helps clear the energetic interference of debt energy, which can hold you back and delay you from going to the next level of prosperity. To amplify your financial flow, state the following energy-healing command: "Increase my financial flow to the highest appropriate level for my greatest and highest good and the greatest and highest good of all concerned." This time the pendulum will start moving in a clockwise direction as it helps increase the potential for greater financial flow. Once your pendulum has finished moving, then you are ready for the next step.

Step 7: Amplify Your Business Presence

With your pendulum in hand, use the following energy-healing command: "Amplify my business presence in the highest and best way to help all who could benefit from my [state product or service]." This time your pendulum will start moving in a clockwise direction as it helps amplify the potential for greater business presence. In this sense, as energy clears you may notice your marketing work becomes more successful and newer opportunities present themselves. Once your pendulum has finished moving, then you are ready for the next step.

Step 8: Raise the Level of Love Energy

With your pendulum in hand, use the following energy-healing command: "Raise the level of love energy within my [state product or service] to the highest appropriate level for the greatest good of all concerned." This time your pendulum will start moving in a clockwise direction as it helps elevate the frequencies of love energy within your product or service. Once your pendulum has finished moving, then you are ready for the next step.

Closing and Grounding Prayer

You always end with a prayer of thanksgiving for the universal support and guidance. The closing and grounding prayer will also help you spiritually and energetically detach from the distance business energy-clearing treatment. The following prayer is an example of what you can use: "Thank you to my divine light team (or to my universal support system) for helping me with this energy-clearing treatment today. Please clear and ground my energy in the highest and best way. I now detach. Thank you. Amen. It is done!"

Well done—you've just completed an amazing distance business energy-clearing treatment!

Next you will find out how to do a distance business premises energy-clearing treatment.

Distance Business Premises Energy–Clearing Protocol

Step 1: Energetic Protection and Connection Prayer (Cocreation)

The following two prayers offer you an example of what you can say. The first prayer is for when you distantly clear the energy of your own business premises, and the second prayer is for when you do a distance business premises energy-clearing treatment for a loved one or friend.

> I ask for divine light protection within and around myself and my business premises as I begin a distance energy-clearing treatment. I ask for divine light support to assist me in every aspect of this energy-clearing treatment, in harmony with my greatest and highest good and the greatest and highest good of my business premises, and all concerned. Thank you. Amen. It is done!

> I ask for divine light protection within and around myself, [state name of loved one / friend], and his/her business premises as I begin a distance energy-clearing treatment. I ask for divine light support to assist me in every aspect of this energy-clearing treatment, in harmony with my greatest and highest good and the greatest and highest good of [state name of loved one / friend], his/her business premises, and all concerned. Thank you. Amen. It is done!

To help empower the prayer request, you can also visualize vibrant white or golden light resonating within and around you. Remember you can adapt these prayers to suit your own creative style and belief system, while also making sure that you still cover asking for energetic protection and spiritual support. Always express gratitude, which greatly amplifies the prayer request.

That's you linked in, switched on, and ready to go!

Step 2: Energy Test to Check If You Can Begin

With the pendulum in hand, ask aloud if it is appropriate to proceed with a distance energy-clearing treatment for [state full business address]. If the pendulum swings back and forth in the yes position, then you will know that it is appropriate to proceed. If the pendulum swings side to side in the no position, then the answer is no, and it's not appropriate to proceed at this time, so don't do it.

Step 3: Measure the Overall Energy of the Business Property

Use the energy measurement chart with your pendulum and ask to be shown the overall energy of the property. Take a note of the measurement.

Step 4: Discern Potential Energy Problems

You can do this step if you want to, by intuitively discerning the overall energy of the business premises and environment. If not, just move on to the next step.

Step 5: Clear the Etheric Energy of the Business Property

With your pendulum in hand, state the following energy-clearing command: "Clear the etheric energy pattern within this property." Your pendulum will start moving in a counterclockwise direction as it clears any energetic issues that do not support the etheric energy pattern of the property. Once your pendulum has finished moving, then you are ready for the next step.

Step 6: Clear the Emotional Energy of the Business Property

With your pendulum in hand, state the following energy-clearing command: "Clear any imbalanced emotional residue within this property." Your pendulum will start moving in a counterclockwise direction as it removes any congested emotional-energy charges that do not support the overall energetic atmosphere of the property. Once your pendulum has finished moving, then you are ready for the next step.

Step 7: Clear the Mental Energy of the Business Property

With your pendulum in hand, state the following energy-clearing command: "Clear any imbalanced mental residue and negative thought forms and images within this property." Your pendulum will start moving in a counterclockwise direction as it removes any congested mental energy charges that include thought forms and mental images that do not support the overall energetic atmosphere of the property. Once your pendulum has finished moving, then you are ready for the next step.

Step 8: Clear the Spiritual Energies of the Business Property

With your pendulum in hand, state the following energy-clearing command: "Clear any nonbeneficial astral and spiritual energies within this property." This covers all four of the property's spiritual energy fields. Your pendulum will start moving in a counterclockwise direction as it removes any nonbeneficial astral and spiritual energies that do not support the overall energetic atmosphere of the property. Once your pendulum has finished moving, then you are ready for the next step.

Step 9: Clear Any Objects and Items of Furniture

When doing a distance business energy-clearing treatment, you will be clearing the energy of any objects or items of furniture within the property in one go and not separately. Use the following energy-clearing command: "Clear the adverse effects of any and all forms of nonbeneficial energy and interference within or attached to any object or item of furniture within this property, originating from all timelines and dimensions of experience." Once your pendulum has finished moving, then you are ready for the next step.

Step 10: Ask If There Is Any Geopathic Stress Adversely Affecting the Property

With your pendulum in hand, ask if there is any geopathic stress adversely affecting this property. If you receive a yes response, then use the following energy-clearing command: "Clear the adverse energetic effects of any geopathic stress interfering with this property and all concerned with the property." Your pendulum will start moving in a counterclockwise direction as it clears the adverse energetic effects of geopathic stress upon the property and all concerned. Once your pendulum has finished moving, then you are ready for the next step.

Step 11: Ask If There Is Any Technological Stress Adversely Affecting the Property

With your pendulum in hand, ask if there is any technological stress adversely affecting this property. If you receive a yes response, then use the following energy-clearing command: "Clear the adverse energetic effects of any technological stress interfering with this property and all concerned." Your pendulum will start moving in a counterclockwise direction as it clears the adverse energetic effects of technological stress upon the property and all concerned. Once your pendulum has finished moving, then you are ready for the next step.

Step 12: Ask If There Are Any Ghost or Spirit Energies in the Property

With your pendulum in hand, ask if there are any ghost or spirit energies in the property. If you receive a yes response, then go ahead and use the following energy-clearing command: "Clear any and all ghost residue or spirit energies within this property. Release and guide any spirits to the Spirit Realm in order that they may continue on with their soul journey, evolution, and development in the highest and best way for the good of all." Your pendulum will start moving in a counterclockwise direction as it clears any ghostly residue and spirit energy within the property. Once your pendulum has finished moving, then you are ready for the next step.

Step 13: Ask If There Are Any Energy Patterns Adversely Affecting the Property

With your pendulum in hand, ask if there are any negative energy patterns adversely affecting the property. If you receive a yes response, then go ahead and use the following energy-clearing command: "Clear any and all negative energy patterns adversely affecting this property and business at their point of origin." Your pendulum will start moving in a counterclockwise direction as it clears the adverse energetic effects of negative energy patterns held within the property.

Step 14: Raise the Level of Love Energy

With your pendulum in hand, use the following energy-healing command: "Raise the level of love energy within this property to the highest appropriate level for the greatest good of all concerned." This time your pendulum will start moving in a clockwise direction as it helps elevate the frequencies of love energy within the property. Once your pendulum has finished moving, then you are ready for the closing prayer.

Closing and Grounding Prayer

The following prayer is an example of what you can use. "Thank you to my divine light team (or to my universal support system) for helping me with this energy-clearing treatment today. Please clear and ground my energy in the highest and best way. I now detach. Thank you. Amen. It is done!"

Well done—you've just completed an amazing distance business premises energy-clearing treatment!

Creative Visualization Energy Technique to Support a Sale of a Property (House or Business)

Two clients of mine contacted me because they had difficulty selling their homes. One home had been on the market for quite some time, while the other home was an inherited home, due to the death of my client's father. It just wouldn't sell. People would book appointments to come see the homes, yet they often didn't show up, or if they did, they were never interested. Both homes remained energetically tied to their owners for different reasons, along with having some energetic issues that caused interference in the overall vibration of the properties. A distance house energy-clearing treatment dealt with these energetic issues, and along with adding in some inspired creative visualizations, it helped transform the energy of both homes to a beneficial state ready to be released to the next suitable owner. The homes could now be seen by the people whose personal energies were a great match for that type of property.

While you already know how to do a distance house/business energy-clearing treatment, the following energy exercise can be added on to the end of a treatment to help you magnetize your intention to sell your property. The creative goal is to simply help you speed up the sale of your home or property, especially if you've had persisting problems with it selling.

CREATIVE EXERCISE TO HELP SELL YOUR PROPERTY

You do not need to use a pendulum for this energy exercise.

Your intention is for your property to be seen by all those who would be a perfect match to purchase it. To help make it "visible" on the "energetic level," which is what helps create and attract a person's intentions into reality, you are going to light up the home with vibrant white light and some other inspired images, state some simple intentions, and then finish with a prayer as follows:

Imagine the entire property completely immersed in vibrant white light (protective light) so that it's glowing bright. Now add in your first intention with clear mental focus: "I intend to sell my property as quickly as I can." With your creative mind, now begin to pulse the white light within and around the property so that it flashes on and off. Next, mentally create a large, bright-yellow neon sign floating above the property that states, "For sale." Now add in your next intention: "I make this property visible to all those who would be a perfect match for it." Next, mentally and emotionally create the following scenario: You've just discovered that you've received an offer on your property, and you are delighted with it. Emotionally feel this good news as you mentally create the picture of you jumping up and down for joy, doing a happy dance or whatever it is you do when you receive great news! Now add in your last intention: "I release this property in the perfect way for the good of all." Finish with the following prayer:

I ask the Light (or the universe, God, angels, etc.) to intervene and help me sell my property to the right family or person that would benefit from it. Please make the property visible to them and guide them to find it in the highest and best way. I ask to receive the best possible offer for my property for the greatest good of all concerned. Thank you. Amen. It is done!

This simple yet powerful prayer will set the universal forces in motion to help you, and especially because you are addressing the greatest good of all concerned. As soon as your property has sold, the creative-energy images and thought forms (mental intentions) that you formed around the property will be dissolved into the energy of joy.

CHAPTER 11

PERSONAL ENERGY– CLEARING TREATMENT
(STEPS AND PROTOCOL)

When a sudden recovery of a patient cannot be explained by medical science, doctors often term such a recovery as a "spontaneous remission" and say in some strange way that "Nature has asserted itself."

—HARRY EDWARDS

Now it's time to begin the process and application of a personal energy-clearing treatment. Just as in chapter 8, you will be guided through the exact steps and then the protocol to complete a personal energy-clearing treatment for yourself and others. A personal energy-clearing treatment can help restore energetic balance, inner peace, and harmony back to your mind, body, and soul. It will help clear the adverse effects of stress, anxiety, and fear energy on your nervous system, body, and soul. Personal energy-clearing treatments can therefore lead toward you experiencing a calmer mind, an empowered immune system, and amplified creative power. We need plenty of creative power to help us attract and create more-beneficial opportunities and life experiences, as well as helping keep us vitally strong. You can return back to this chapter again and again until the energy-clearing protocols become second nature. The majority of all personal energy-clearing treatments are done as a distance energy-clearing treatment. You can therefore work from the comfort of your own home when helping another, which is great news if your loved one or friend happens to live in a different country. Other times, however, including your personal preference, you can also do a personal energy-clearing treatment with the person sitting close by or with the person interacting with you live on video sharing. In this case, they would sit nearby or share a screen with you as you go through the energy-clearing protocol. You may actually receive more-intuitive impressions when you work in this way because you are close enough to be immersed within their auric field if sitting nearby and because you will be consciously connected to them if sharing a screen. You can then let them know anything you intuitively sense, and they can offer you any feedback as you work through the protocol. Both ways of working are just as good and viable as the other, and you may find that you do prefer one way over another. Allow your intuition to guide you and be creative as you move through the energy-clearing protocols.

Personal Energy–Clearing Treatment (Self and Others)

When doing a personal energy-clearing treatment, it's always best to do so when you feel that you are emotionally balanced, and when you know that you won't be interrupted. Note: if you don't want to use a pendulum to energy-test, measure energy, and help clear energy, then you can simply use the necessary energy-clearing prayer commands found in the protocol section, combined with your intuition.

Prior to beginning a distance personal energy-clearing treatment for someone else, take a note of their full name, age, and location. This will help you zone directly into their unique vibrational frequency and spiritual coordinates. If the person is sitting nearby or is sharing a live screen with you, then you will be visually and energetically connecting to them. The steps and protocol are exactly the same for either a distance energy-clearing treatment or if you are working on yourself or on someone nearby.

PERSONAL ENERGY–CLEARING STEPS (SELF AND OTHERS)

Step 1: Energetic Protection and Connection Prayer (Cocreation)

Always begin with a prayer for energetic protection and for spiritual connection to help you connect with and direct the universal clearing/healing forces of Divine Love and Light. When doing a personal energy-clearing treatment for someone else, it is always best to ask their permission to do so, just in case they don't want you interfering with their energy and consciousness.

Step 2: Energy Test to Check If You Can Begin

You will be using the pendulum to ask aloud if it is appropriate to proceed with an energy-clearing treatment for [state full name of person or say for yourself]. If the pendulum swings back and forth in the yes position, then you will know that it is appropriate to proceed. You don't need to make it any more difficult than this. If the answer is no, then it's not appropriate to proceed at this time, so don't do it. Reasons for a no response can be because you are dehydrated, you are overly tired (your energies may have switched polarities), or you may lack confidence in your ability to do so, or it can simply be because the energy of the person or yourself doesn't require an energy-clearing treatment at this specific time. Have a glass of water to rehydrate, do an energy-balancing technique (chapter 7), and ask again or simply leave it and ask again at a different time. If you don't want to use a pendulum to energy-test to check if it's appropriate for you to proceed, then you can either do a sway test or a finger test or simply just rely on your intuition for a yes/no response.

Step 3: Measure the Overall Energy of You or Another

Use the energy measurement chart (chapter 7) with your pendulum and ask to be shown the overall energy of "you" or the "person" you are doing an energy clearing for, by stating their full name. The energy measurement chart provides a simple way to discern the overall energy frequency of a person, a pet, a place, an object, etc., helping you detect and discern the difference between a range of low- and high-vibe frequencies. Prior to measuring your or another's energy, it is important to note that there is nothing to be alarmed about if the reading is low and falls in the negative range on the left-hand side of the chart. Remember that you are measuring a person's energy only from a spiritual and energetic perspective. You are not diagnosing any physical or mental health issues; you are simply measuring a person's energy to help address any energetic imbalances. Energy fluctuates and changes with people's current emotional states, life challenges, past traumas, past and present fears, day-to-day stress, etc., and this is separate to any external nonbeneficial energy factors and forces that can also cause interference. When I worked in the psychiatric hospital, I was so fatigued because of the heavy, dense, low vibrational environment. My overall energy would have measured on the left-hand side of the chart, falling somewhere within the negative low-vibe range. While my physical health was strong, my energy level was certainly low, and therefore testing low doesn't mean there will be a significant health concern.

The majority of health issues tend to begin at an energetic level first before they manifest their imbalance within the physical body. This even accounts for hereditary factors within the DNA or within epigenetics, and with our soul history. Illness, disease, aches, and pains are more often than not due to accumulated energetic imbalances that first begin within our energy bodies, systems, and fields. Other times, external life factors, toxins, viruses, bacteria, and physical neglect of the body's needs can be the primary concern. Yet, energy clearings can help empower the immune system to deal with these external issues in combination with any medical intervention. Regular energy clearings are extremely beneficial in clearing, correcting, rebalancing, and resolving any accumulated imbalances from a spiritual and energetic perspective, and they can therefore help prevent the discordant energy frequencies from moving into the physical body and manifesting dis-ease. In this sense, energy clearings as well as all forms of spiritual and energetic healing can often be thought of as preventive medicine. This doesn't mean that you should choose energy-clearing treatments over medical diagnosis and assistance; on the contrary, there is outstanding medical treatment and medication that can save lives and extend lives. What it does mean is that you have another way to help yourself and others, and this way is the spiritual and energetic way. A cool combination of medical and energetic treatment can be a win-win situation all around.

When measuring the overall energy of you or another, typically anything measuring between 75 and 100 percent falls into the "high-vibe/healthy" range, meaning that the overall energy vibrations of what's being measured are already in pretty good shape and will require a minimal amount of energy clearing. In this sense, when you go through the energy-clearing steps with the pendulum, it may spin for only a short period of time (seconds), and some steps may not be required at all. Anything measuring between 50 and 75 percent falls into the "strong-vibe/positive" range and generally indicates energetic residue and imbalances, yet nothing overly problematic. The closer the measurement of something leans toward 75 percent, the higher vibrational strength it will resonate. Anything measuring between 25 and 50 percent falls into the "weak-vibe/negative" range and generally indicates that the person has sufficient energetic concerns at this time. When going through the energy-clearing protocol, the pendulum may take much longer when in clearing mode, spinning for maybe a minute or so at a time. Further energy-clearing treatments will probably also be required until the overall energy of the person eventually shifts into higher vibrational resonance and balance and then continues to hold that balance. This is because beneficial energetic shifts will hold and maintain their higher vibrational resonance for only so long when there are still preexisting energetic concerns with the person that often require more time to be fully resolved. Anything measuring from 0 to 25 percent falls into the "low-vibe/negative" range and generally indicates an accumulation of energy problems or one main and critical issue. These problems and issues can be due to trauma memories and energy patterns, probable spiritual interference, and the likes of geopathic stress. However, if you ask if it is okay for you to proceed with the energy-clearing treatment and you get a yes response from the pendulum, then all you need to do is to go through the protocol, applying each step to make the necessary energetic adjustments, and you will surely help the overall energy of yourself or the person to shift, lift, and increase in its vibrational resonance.

You are always working with unlimited universal support to help you, and you aren't doing it in your own creative power. When your or another person's vibration is significantly low and falls in the negative range (it will never be 0 percent), it can mean that there may also be energy problems within the home or work environment. It will be a good idea to measure the energy of the home/work environment to check on whether there are any significant energy concerns there that can also be dealt with. An energy clearing of their home/work environment will also help support your or their personal energy fields.

If you don't want to use a pendulum and chart to measure the overall energetic frequency of yourself or another, then just trust and rely on your intuition to discern how the overall energy of yourself or another feels to you.

Step 4: Clear the Etheric Energy Body

This aspect of the energy clearing addresses clearing the body's etheric energy structure and the etheric energy pattern of the body's organs, systems, and parts. The energetic intelligence of our spiritual and physical DNA resides within the cells that form the matrix of the etheric energy body. An energy clearing of the etheric energy body can therefore help clear the cellular system of discordant frequencies that can predispose us to illness, dysfunction, and disease. In this sense it will help clear any nonbeneficial energy preparing to resonate within the physical form that may adversely affect the optimal flow and function of the body's physical homeostasis, equilibrium, and vital energetic balance.

I was asked by the mother of a disabled adult woman if I would do a distance energy-clearing treatment to help her with her daily seizures. She explained that her daughter was having blackouts between two and five times a day. The doctors told the daughter that they think it's neurological, and say that they can't do anything for it. They increased her blood pressure tablets, but it made no difference. I went ahead and did the energy clearing and healing treatment, and within a period of twenty-four hours the daughter's seizures completely stopped. What was interesting about this case was that an energy clearing of the etheric energy body helped rebalance the electrical, magnetic, and chemical energies within her body, and then her nervous system responded favorably. The energies of her brain were in sync and her seizures stopped. The rest of the energy-clearing protocol helped keep her overall energies in a higher elevated frequency and therefore maintained the beneficial results. Within a few weeks of this mother's request, I was again asked to help another lady in her forties who was also experiencing seizures. Again, within a period of twenty-four hours her seizures stopped. What I have found to be true is that energy-clearing and healing treatments are an invaluable form of spiritual assistance to a person's health and well-being, and especially when medical science is unable to unravel the underlying cause or to help ease the physical symptoms.

Step 5: Clear the Emotional Energy Body

This aspect of the energy clearing addresses clearing any imbalanced emotional charges, ranging from very recent to those that have accumulated over longer periods of time, even going as far back as childhood or to being a baby in the womb. Sadness, depression, anxiety, overwhelmingness, guilt, anger, frustration, and irritation, along with different trauma memories, all can leave their emotional imprints and energetic residue within the emotional energy body. Clearing the emotional energy body therefore clears what is ready to be released from a person's emotional history. Energy clears in layers, and sometimes (not always) it can take time to clear deep emotional pain garnered from traumatic energies, which will most likely clear a little at a time when you do further energy-clearing treatments. You or another will clear only what you are truly ready to process, release, and resolve. The emotional energy body can also at times be triggered by other people's emotions. In this sense the body's auric field, including the emotional body, will have absorbed emotional energy charges originating from others. An energy clearing will clear the emotional body and auric field of this congestion. Emotional charges originating from our ancestor timeline and our soul history timeline can also interfere with the equilibrium of our emotional energy body, due to the unresolved emotional pain and trauma memories. An energy clearing of the emotional body can help you or another feel much lighter and brighter in disposition and joy.

Step 6: Clear the Mental Energy Body

This aspect of the energy clearing addresses clearing your or another's mental energy body of any imbalanced thoughts, images, and visions due to the misdirected use of our powerful imagination and ego mind. This is often due to us worrying and obsessing over certain life challenges, worrying about our loved ones, and stressing about the future and what may be. Angry words spoken due to arguments can also create nonbeneficial mental residue within our mental energy body. Our imagination and thought power can create images, shapes, and color that can appear within the energetic atmosphere of our mental energy body. Our mental energy body can become easily congested by overanalyzing something. An energy fog will form and surround the head and shoulders as an expression of this congestion. Clearing the mental energy body can lift this energetic fog and help restore greater clarity of mind and inner peace; the latter, being beneficial for sleeping, since an overworked mind will find it difficult to switch off and relax into a deep sleep. Clearing the mental energy body will also help clear the adverse energetic effects of our limiting beliefs about our self, others, and the world in which we live. It can help us regain our confidence and restore our personal power, since we will have the presence of mind to reexamine our belief system. Another factor of mental energetic imbalance is when we are overly indecisive and unable to make reasonable decisions without fretting or without wanting someone else to make up our minds for us. An energy clearing can help us regain the clarity and confidence around decision-making by helping us become in touch with our natural intuitive nature and gut instinct. Our mental energy body is also influenced by the thoughts and beliefs of our heritage, culture, and environment. Just like we may carry certain family traditions, we can also carry certain limiting beliefs and patterns that did not originate with us. When we clear our mental energy body, we can begin to clear these limiting energies and negative patterns so that we will regain more of our soul's creative power. When we amplify our soul's creative power, we will have more spiritual presence and freedom of mind to attract and create greater opportunities and more-rewarding life experiences. Other people's mental impressions can also affect us, whether this is done intentionally or unintentionally. Anger energy as well as hate energy being directed toward us can interfere with our auric field and mental energy body. Energy weapons, due to someone's creative mental force, can enter into the auric field and can take the etheric shape of daggers, pointed arrows, hooks, and other etheric anomalies. These will disturb the auric field and interfere with the energetic balance and equilibrium of our overall personal energies and even negatively affect the physical body. The mental energy body can also be compromised by the adverse effects of negative subliminal influences and suggestions, and therefore a clearing of the mental energy body can help clear these destructive and protruding mental programs and influences upon us. Overall, an energy clearing of the mental body can help you or another feel empowered and confident, with greater clarity of mind, as well as helping strengthen your intuitive nature and to trust in your own free-will decisions.

Step 7: Clear the Spiritual Energy Bodies (Four Spiritual Bodies/Fields)

This aspect of the energy clearing addresses clearing any imbalanced astral and spiritual energies that can adversely affect you or another, such as unknown energetic anomalies, astral fragments, and spiritual interference that do not originate from this realm. The first of the four spiritual fields is associated with the heart and soul energy of the body, since it holds the energy frequencies of unconditional love, inner peace, and harmony. This heart and soul energy is what enables us to stay harmonious and strong and is a rock for us when we are going through personal life challenges and temporary struggles. When the heart and soul energy is compromised by an array of energetic imbalances, it lowers the body's overall vibrational frequency. Immune function can become compromised, personal relationships with others can become strained, and financial situations and life experiences can become troublesome, since the harmony within the heart and soul is disturbed. The heart and soul energy is intimately associated with the energies of creation and with our higher mental energy body, the causal body. Imbalanced creative forces within us concerning giving and receiving energy to and from the universe are what can interfere with the energetic exchanges we share with our personal and family relationships and with our financial flow, due to the resistance we have in aligning with an ever-abundant universe. An energy clearing can help clear this resistance, which can be multilayered and will clear a little at a time, due to the many imbalances that can affect us at a heart and soul level. The heart level carries our trauma memories from this lifetime and from our ancestor energies. The soul level carries trauma memories from our soul history throughout Creation. This is why we have many unhealed and unresolved trauma energies that we aren't even consciously aware of. We will clear only what we are ready to process, resolve, and let go of. Yet, every energy clearing enables us to return back toward our unlimited spiritual nature and authentic Spirit.

The second of the four spiritual fields includes the body's perfect blueprint pattern of the body's original intent, purpose, and design. It is continuously projected to the etheric energy of the body to help spiritually and energetically sustain the physical form. There is also higher energetic maintenance and spiritual support from the next two spiritual fields that help oversee the body's nervous system and functions. Part of this spiritual support is known as the body's higher self. A low vibration of and within the body doesn't necessarily stop this support of our higher self; it simply weakens it. When this weakness happens, the body and consciousness are made more vulnerable to astral and spiritual interference. Astral interference derives its energies from the lower astral realms, which is the closest in frequency to this dense world of matter. It can also include the psychic energy of the living (their misdirected thought forms). Such interference can manifest as persisting problems with the well-being of the body and consciousness. Maybe when one issue is dealt with, another one quickly arises. Spiritual interference can be due to earthbound spirit attachments or influence, yet this can be easily rectified with a personal energy-clearing treatment. Applying this energy-clearing command is like removing invisible energetic debris that lacks the love vibration. Immediately the energy of the body can return to a more balanced and harmonious state. It's not that you are directly dealing with or removing earthbound spirits at this point, yet if there are any adversely affecting you or another, then you will be clearing their energetic spiritual residue. This energy-clearing step, covering the four spiritual fields, is extraordinary, and all it takes is your mental focus, concentration, and cocreation with the Light, and you will help restore the heart and soul energy of the body, empower the body's immune function, and more clearly align with the higher self.

Step 8: Check, Clear, and Bless the Chakras (Seven Energy Centers)

This remarkable energy-clearing step enables you to check on the condition of each of the seven main energy centers to see whether they require an energy clearing and blessing. This simple process can instigate impressive transformational shifts within the body's endocrine system, within our nervous system, and with our psychological health and well-being. The chakra system, located within our etheric energy body, is the spiritual map and celestial key to our healing, creative expansion, and spiritual growth. Our consciousness expands through the transformation of our limited perceptions and through an understanding and application of higher spiritual knowledge. The chakra system enables us to work with each individual energy center that governs over the body's organs, systems, and body parts. By clearing and blessing these energy centers, it helps restore optimal energetic flow and function to the chakras and to the areas of the body that they energetically govern and feed. As a spiritual healer, I've observed amazing results occur with people's health and life when their chakras are cleared and blessed. While previously congested energetic valves reopen within us to improve our physical health and well-being, new doors of opportunity can also open within our external environment. Why? Because the chakras are portals of Light with great significance in our ability to attract and create an extraordinary life experience.

Step 9: Clear the Adverse Energetic Effects of Other People's Energies

This aspect of the personal energy-clearing treatment is invaluable in helping remove other people's energies and influences that negatively impinge on you or another. Other people's energies can adversely affect your energy levels and can impinge on your consciousness by negatively influencing your thoughts and emotions. While some of these energies are cleared away from you when you do the emotional and mental body energy-clearing commands, it is also extremely useful to include this one in as an extra energetic measure. If our aura is congested by a mix of our own energetic stressors, then we will naturally weaken our auric resistance to spiritual and energetic protection. In this case, we can become more susceptible and vulnerable to absorbing the negative energies of others. When this happens, our aura is further congested. We can experience the results of this as major fatigue, irritability, depressed thoughts, or emotional swings. A simple energy clearing can help clear our aura of congestion and clear the negative influences upon us so that we remain within our own energetic boundaries.

Step 10: Clear the Adverse Energetic Effects of Any Negative Subliminal Energies or Suggestions

This energy-clearing step enables us to be free and clear of any untoward negative suggestions or subliminal influences that do not serve our greatest and highest good. We are constantly bombarded with advertisements and disinformation from the media, news, and online presence. Some of this is nonbeneficial to our consciousness, and if our aura is already somewhat weakened and we aren't fully grounded within our own energy and consciousness, then we can become more easily compromised and influenced. This specific energy-clearing command is one that will clear you or another of this negative interference.

Step 11: Clear the Adverse Energetic Effects of the Collective Consciousness

This energy-clearing step will help clear the collective energy of fear upon you or another. Fear energy is created from the collective mind of humanity and can impinge on our own consciousness to heighten any fear energy we have within us. We all have different degrees of irrational fear energy within us; even those people on the planet who have gained high levels of spiritual growth have remnants of unresolved irrational fear energy within them. Our spiritual growth does not stop with this incarnation. Irrational fear within us always stems from our ego mind, which believes it is separate from Source. We have enough to deal with, with our own fearful insecurities, without needing to take on more from the collective. Remember that energy is impressed upon matter, and the collective fear energy of humanity is also impressed upon the planet, upon the environment, and upon weather conditions. Collective fear, collective anger, and all the other collective low vibrational emotional and mental outpourings can disturb the natural balance of the earth's magnetic field, which can then cause energetic problems with all of Earth's inhabitants.

Step 12: Ask If There Is Any Psychic or Spiritual Interference Adversely Affecting You or Another (Includes Nonbeneficial Energy Cords)

In this energy-clearing step, you are going to ask the pendulum to check if there is any psychic or spiritual interference adversely affecting you or another. It is your spiritual support system that will be checking on this for you, and if there is any, then they will also be dealing with it as you do the energy-clearing command found in the protocol section. Psychic interference can be nothing more than unintentional negative thoughts about you that is impinging on your energy field and consciousness. It typically manifests as headaches that don't improve with pain relief. However, through keeping your vibration strong and high vibe, you will very rarely be affected by psychic interference in this way because a higher vibration will always override a lower one. If your energy is already compromised and weakened, then it is possible for you to be adversely affected in this way. This is why the previous energy-clearing steps help clear any nonbeneficial energies that do not belong to you, in order for you to keep your energy and aura nice and strong, balanced, and in general good shape. An intentional psychic attack often falls into the spiritual-interference category because it is intentional. This means that if a person wants to cause you harm, and by whatever method they've chosen to do so, it is done at a psychic and spiritual level. Maybe they've instigated some form of black magic on you or another, or maybe they've wished you harm with a great deal of mental focus and intent. Intentional spiritual interference can be minor to major in its manifestation, and some of these results can manifest as persisting illness when the medical world can't find anything wrong, or periods of ongoing bad luck. A simple energy clearing with your spiritual support system can clear any intentional or unintentional psychic or spiritual interference. Plus, as I've previously mentioned, when keeping your energy high vibe, you will be very rarely affected in this way. When it comes to energy lines (cords of attachment), this step helps clear any negative energy and congestion formed between people, and dissolves old energy lines from previous relationships that are no longer together and active. Exampled of such are when a person separates from and divorces their partner, previous sexual relationships that have ended, and traumatic and abusive relationships.

Step 13: Ask If There Are Any Spirit Energies or Attachments Adversely Affecting You or Another

There is nothing to fear in clearing and releasing spirits, since you are working in cocreation with the Light and your spiritual support system. Spirit energies can include attached fragmented soul energies that still have consciousness, or actual spirit beings with active consciousness. Since you are working in harmony with your universal backup system, these spirit energies will be guided to the Spirit realm in the highest and best way, and any soul fragments will be returned to their source once energetically cleared.

Step 14: Ask If There Are Any Negative Energy Patterns Adversely Affecting You or Another

By clearing negative energy patterns at their point of origin, you will begin to help weaken and dissolve them. Energy patterns can be multilayered, and each time that you do an energy-clearing treatment, you will help lessen their adverse effects on your consciousness until they are finally resolved. An example of a negative energy pattern is a destructive habit or addiction. Each personal energy clearing can help bring the habit pattern and addiction into moderation, since it weakens the desire and triggers associated with the habit or addiction. A strong desire for something builds its own energetic field, which is what helps lock the habit or addiction in place. By clearing these energetic fields through utilizing this energy-clearing command, you help support you or another in overcoming any personal challenges. This step can help you or another gain the willpower and strength to break through destructive habit patterns. A habit pattern can also be expressed as negative and critical thinking of self and others, such as constant complaining about conditions in life, which sadly creates more resistance around whatever a person complains about, so that it locks the limiting conditions in place—which again triggers further complaints. This is a wonderful energy-clearing step to include in order to help yourself or others with issues that have become imbalanced.

Step 15: Clear Any and All Disease Frequencies Adversely Affecting You or Another

This step is included because everything has an energetic frequency, including different diseases. If our overall energy is of a high-enough vibration, then we are less likely to be adversely affected by disease frequencies, although not always, since life sometimes throws us a curveball. If we do happen to be affected by some form of disease, then this energy-clearing step can support our immune system and body to do what it needs in order to defend and rebalance itself. This step can also provide aid as a form of preventive energetic care for the body, since it helps energetically clear any potential disease frequencies that we may be about to succumb to.

Step 16: Raise the Level of Love Energy within Every Cell of Your or Another's Physical Body to the Highest Appropriate Level

This is an amazing "energy healing" command to use, since it helps integrate, process, and transform all the previous energy-clearing steps. While the previous steps will have already begun to raise the vibrational frequency of you or another, by raising the level of love energy within every cell of the body, it will help empower physical health and well-being. You are increasing beneficial energy within the body to help sustain and maintain the results of the energy-clearing treatment.

Step 17: Bless the Immune System and Harmonize It with the Physical Body

This step is a creative healing prayer command that will help rebalance and empower the body's immune system and harmonize it with the physical body so that it works for it and not against it. It is a wonderful healing command to use that can support the physical body to heal itself. Our immune system works for us to defend us against disease in the same way that our aura works for us to defend us against nonbeneficial energies and frequencies. If our immune system is out of balance, it will work against the body, as is the case with autoimmune diseases. This step can help you energetically correct this imbalance so that it reverts back to the job it was originally and divinely designed to do.

One personal energy-clearing treatment can do only so much, and so regular clearing treatments, every month or so, will aid in further energetic corrections and transformations until eventually you notice improvements or complete resolution of any persisting issues. We live in a constant sea of energetic exchanges, and this is the main reason why regular energy-clearing treatments are super beneficial.

HOW TO FINISH THE PERSONAL ENERGY–CLEARING TREATMENT: THREE SEPARATE STEPS:

Here are three final steps to help you complete the personal energy-clearing treatment.

Step 1: Clear the Adverse Energetic Effects of the Surrounding Area, Neighborhood, and the Community on You or Another

This step simply helps clear any external energy problems that may be causing a disturbance with your or another's overall vibration.

Step 2: Clear, Bless, and Empower the Auric Field of You or Another

This step clears any interference or congestion within the main auric field. Blessing the aura will also empower the protective energy field surrounding you or another so that it can deflect any potential harm.

Step 3: Remeasure the Overall Energy of You or Another

Now that you've successfully completed a personal energy-clearing treatment, you can go ahead and remeasure the overall energy of you or another to check if it's increased in vibrational resonance. If it has, then great news; just keep a check on it every month or so. If there is no elevated change in the overall vibration when you remeasure, then you need to give it more time, because while energetic shifts take place immediately on a spiritual level, they often take more time to process on a dense and physical level, and therefore results can emerge and keep improving over a period of twenty-four hours and beyond. The good news is that if you have completed all or most of the steps in the personal energy-clearing protocol, then you will most certainly notice energetic improvements, even if they do take time. The tangible results of the elevated energy vibration that you or another is now experiencing can include increased energy levels, greater clarity of mind, improvements, or total resolution of persisting health issues, aches, and pains. Elevated levels of inner peace and joy. Harmonious relationships. Feeling more emotionally balanced for longer periods of time. Life challenges are easier to deal with and overcome. New beneficial opportunities present themselves for further life experiences, soul growth, creative expansion, and fulfillment.

Closing and Grounding Prayer

Just as you prayed to begin the personal energy-clearing treatment, so do you pray to end it. In this sense you help detach your energy from the protocol and ground and rebalance your own energetic equilibrium. It is also a way to offer thanksgiving to your universal support system.

Now that you've read through each step, you are ready to begin the personal energy-clearing protocol.

Personal Energy-Clearing Protocol (Self or Another)

Step 1: Energetic Protection and Connection Prayer (Cocreation)

The first prayer is for when you clear your own energy, and the second prayer is for when you clear the energy of another.

I ask for divine light protection within and around me as I begin an energy-clearing treatment. I ask for divine light support to assist me in every aspect of my energy-clearing treatment, in harmony with my greatest and highest good and the greatest and highest good of all concerned. Thank you. Amen. It is done!

I ask for divine light protection within and around myself and [state full name of loved one / friend] as I begin an energy-clearing treatment. I ask for divine light support to assist me in every aspect of [state full name of loved one / friend]'s energy-clearing treatment today, in harmony with my greatest and highest good, [state full name of loved one/friend]'s greatest and highest good, and the greatest and highest good of all concerned. Thank you. Amen. It is done!

To help empower the prayer request, you can also visualize vibrant white or golden light resonating within and around you as you do the energy-clearing treatment. You can also adapt these prayers to suit your own creative style and belief system, while also making sure that you still cover asking for energetic protection and spiritual support. Always express gratitude, which greatly amplifies the prayer request.

That's you linked in, switched on, and ready to go!

Step 2: Energy Test to Check If You Can Begin

With the pendulum in hand, ask aloud if it is appropriate to proceed with an energy-clearing treatment for yourself or for [state full name of loved one / friend]. If you are doing a distance energy-clearing treatment for another, then also use their location and age to zone right into their specific frequency and spiritual coordinates. Example: "Is it appropriate to proceed with an energy-clearing treatment for Cheryl Fraser, forty-nine, Inverness, Scotland?"

Step 3: Measure the Overall Energy of You or Another

Use the energy measurement chart with your pendulum and ask to be shown the overall energy of you or another. Take a note of the measurement.

Step 4: Clear the Etheric Energy Body

With your pendulum in hand, state the following energy-clearing command: "Clear my (or another's) etheric energy body." Your pendulum will start moving in a counterclockwise direction as it clears or corrects any energetic issues that are causing problems with the etheric energy body. Once your pendulum has finished moving, then you are ready for the next step.

Step 5: Clear the Emotional Energy Body

With your pendulum in hand, state the following energy-clearing command: "Clear my (or another's) emotional body of any imbalanced or congested emotions." Your pendulum will start moving in a counterclockwise direction as it removes any imbalanced or congested emotional energy charges. Once your pendulum has finished moving, then you are ready for the next step.

Step 6: Clear the Mental Energy Body

With your pendulum in hand, state the following energy-clearing command: "Clear my (or another's) mental body of any congestion and negative thought forms and images." Your pendulum will start moving in a counterclockwise direction as it removes any congested mental energy charges that include negative thought forms and mental images. Once your pendulum has finished moving, then you are ready for the next step.

Step 7: Clear the Spiritual Energy Bodies (Astral, Etheric Template, Celestial, and Causal)

With your pendulum in hand, state the following energy-clearing command: "Clear all four spiritual bodies of any nonbeneficial astral and spiritual energies." This covers all four of your or another's spiritual energy bodies and fields. Your pendulum will start moving in a counterclockwise direction as it removes any nonbeneficial astral and spiritual energies. Once your pendulum has finished moving, then you are ready for the next step.

Step 8: Check, Clear, and Bless the Chakras (Seven Energy Centers)

With your pendulum in hand, state the following question: "Does my (or another's) base chakra require a clearing?" If the answer is no, then move on to the next chakra: "Does my (or another's) sacral plexus chakra require a clearing?" If the answer is yes, then use the following energy-clearing command: "Clear any energetic imbalances and congestion within my sacral plexus chakra." Your pendulum will start moving in a counterclockwise direction as it clears any energetic issues. Once your pendulum has finished moving, then you are ready to bless the chakra. Use the following energy-blessing command: "Bless and restore optimal energetic flow and function to and through the sacral plexus chakra." This time, your pendulum will start moving in a clockwise direction as it blesses and restores chakra power. Check, clear, and bless the chakras from the base to the crown, if required.

Step 9: Clear the Adverse Energetic Effects of Other People's Energies

With your pendulum in hand, use the following energy-clearing command: "Clear, neutralize, remove, and resolve the adverse energetic effects of other people's energies upon my (or another's) entire system." Your pendulum will begin to move in a counterclockwise direction as it clears the interference. Once your pendulum has finished moving, then you are ready for the next step.

Step 10: Clear the Adverse Energetic Effects of Any Negative Subliminal Energies or Suggestions

With your pendulum in hand, use the following energy-clearing command: "Clear, neutralize, remove, and resolve the adverse energetic effects of any negative subliminal energies or suggestions upon my (or another's) entire system." Your pendulum will begin to move in a counterclockwise direction as it clears the interference. Once your pendulum has finished moving, then you are ready for the next step.

Step 11: Clear the Adverse Energetic Effects of the Collective Consciousness

With your pendulum in hand, use the following energy-clearing command: "Clear, neutralize, remove, and resolve the adverse energetic effects of the collective consciousness upon my (or another's) entire system." Your pendulum will begin to move in a counterclockwise direction as it clears the interference. Once your pendulum has finished moving, then you are ready for the next step.

Step 12: Ask If There Is Any Psychic or Spiritual Interference Adversely Affecting You or Another (Includes Nonbeneficial Energy Cords)

With your pendulum in hand, use the following energy-clearing command: "Clear, neutralize, remove, and resolve the adverse energetic effects of any psychic or spiritual interference and any negative energy cords upon my (or another's) entire system." Your pendulum will begin to move in a counterclockwise direction as it clears the interference. Once your pendulum has finished moving, then you are ready for the next step.

Step 13: Ask If There Are Any Spirit Energies Attached to You or Another

With your pendulum in hand, ask if there are spirit energies attached to you or another. If you receive a yes response, then go ahead and use the following energy-clearing command: "Clear any and all spirit energies attached to me (or another). Release and guide any spirits to the Spirit Realm in order that they may continue on with their soul journey, evolution, and development in the highest and best way for the good of all." Your pendulum will start moving in a counterclockwise direction as it clears any spirit residue adversely affecting you or another, and as it releases any earthbound spirits and attachments to the Light. Once your pendulum has finished moving, then you are ready for the next step.

Step 14: Ask If There Are Any Negative Energy Patterns Adversely Affecting You or Another

With your pendulum in hand, ask if there are any negative energy patterns adversely affecting you or another. If you receive a yes response, then go ahead and use the following energy-clearing command: "Clear any and all negative energy patterns adversely affecting me (or another) at their point of origin." Your pendulum will start moving in a counterclockwise direction as it clears the adverse energetic effects of negative energy patterns resonating within you. Once your pendulum has finished moving, then you are ready for the next step.

Step 15: Clear Any and All Disease Frequencies Adversely Affecting You or Another

With your pendulum in hand, state the following energy-clearing command: "Clear and neutralize any and all disease frequencies that may be adversely affecting me (or another)." Your pendulum will begin to move in a counterclockwise direction as it clears and neutralizes any and all disease frequencies. Once your pendulum has finished moving, then you are ready for the next step.

Step 16: Raise the Level of Love Energy within Every Cell of Your or Another's Physical Body to the Highest Appropriate Level

With your pendulum in hand, use the following energy-healing command: "Raise the level of love energy within every cell of my (or another's) body to the highest appropriate level for my (or another's) greatest and highest good." This time your pendulum will start moving in a clockwise direction as it helps elevate the frequencies of love energy within every cell of the body. Once your pendulum has finished moving, then you are ready for the next step.

Step 17: Bless the Immune System and Harmonize It with the Physical Body

With your pendulum in hand, use the following energy-healing command: "Bless my (or another's) immune system with optimal energetic flow and function and harmonize it with my (or another's) physical body in the highest and best way."

This time your pendulum will start moving in a clockwise direction as it helps correct, empower, and harmonize the energy of the body's immune system. Once your pendulum has finished moving, then you are ready for the next step.

How to Finish the Personal Energy–Clearing Treatment: Three Separate Steps

Step 1: Clear the Adverse Energetic Effects of the Surrounding Area, Neighborhood, and the Community on You or Another

With your pendulum in hand, state the following energy-clearing command: "Clear the adverse energetic effects of the surrounding area, neighborhood, and community on me (or another)." The pendulum will begin to move in a counterclockwise direction as it clears the external nonbeneficial energies. Once your pendulum has finished moving, then you are ready for the next step.

Step 2: Clear, Bless, and Empower the Auric Field of You or Another

With your pendulum in hand, state the following energy-clearing command: "Clear my (or another's) auric field of all forms of nonbeneficial energies, nonbeneficial frequencies, interference, and harm." The pendulum will begin to move in a counterclockwise direction as it clears the nonbeneficial energies. Then state the following blessing: "Bless my (or another's) aura with a shield of divine light protection for my (or another's) greatest and highest good." This time the pendulum will begin to move in a clockwise direction. Once your pendulum has finished moving, then you are ready for the third step.

Step 3: Remeasure the Overall Energy of You or Another

Take a note of the measurement to check on any improvements in the overall energy of you or another.

Closing and Grounding Prayer

The following prayer is an example of what you can use. "Thank you to my divine light team (or to my universal support system) for helping me with my (or another's) energy-clearing treatment today. Please clear and ground (another's) energy in the highest and best way. They are now detached. Please clear and ground my energy in the highest and best way. I now detach. Thank you. Amen. It is done!"

Note: You need to add another person's name in only if you are doing them a personal energy-clearing treatment. Otherwise, it's just your own name.

Well done—you've just completed an amazing personal energy-clearing treatment!

CHAPTER 12

ENERGY–CLEARING PROTOCOLS FOR CHILDREN, PETS, AND MORE!

No one is useless in this world who lightens the burdens of another.
—Charles Dickens

Distance Treatments for Children

Children do not need a complete energy-clearing treatment in the same way as adults do, because their systems are still young and developing. Yet, they certainly do benefit from energy-clearing treatments because at times they can absorb the stress energies of their parents. They may also experience different concerns and issues as they age, such as nightmares, fear of the dark, sleep problems, learning difficulties, etc. Other times, children may be hyperactive and overly sensitive to the energies within their environment. Children often experience a range of illnesses and problems due to their close connection with their childhood friends and from what's making the rounds in school. Colds, flu, tonsillitis, ear infections, chicken pox, etc. all can be energetically cleared as a way of supporting the child's overall vibration, which then empowers the child's immune system. Obviously, any kind of energy-clearing treatment to help a child overcome their illness or issue from a spiritual and energetic perspective is always done in harmony with any necessary medical care. Also, it's a good idea to do an energy-clearing treatment of their bedroom, since this can help calm their nervous system and help them sleep. There is no need to do an energy-clearing treatment on a baby (unless they are very sick), since the baby is immersed within the mother's energy field. It is actually more beneficial to do an energy-clearing treatment for the mother, and, at times, also for the father, as a way to energetically support them. Babies and small children will benefit greatly from the home environment being energetically cleared. Yet, if you feel you would like to do an energy-clearing treatment on your baby or toddler, then know that your spiritual support system will take care of their energy-clearing needs in the highest and best way. It will certainly be a much-gentler process than that of an adult.

I did a distance energy-clearing treatment for Lewis, a young boy of twelve who'd hurt his right foot during a karate class. He'd been to the hospital for an x-ray, and they said it was a stress fracture. His foot was painful, and he couldn't put any pressure on it. He was bandaged up and was given crutches. These are his own words: "I went to bed that night and I couldn't get to sleep. At about 11 p.m. I felt a sharp pain in my right foot. It lasted for about ten seconds and then it went away, and I fell asleep. When I awoke in the morning, my foot felt much better, and I could put pressure on it. I told my mom, and she said that I'd had an energy-clearing treatment from Joanne. Mom told me that Joanne did the energy clearing at the exact same time that I felt the pain in my foot, which then left. I was happy I could go back to karate and carry on enjoying my classes.

The good news is that children do tend to heal faster than adults because they are less energetically overwhelmed and stressed. The following shortened energy-clearing protocol for children can help your child or another child clear their fear, restore their joy, and rebalance their overall energy. If, however, you intuitively feel guided to add in any steps that you've already learned in all of the other energy-clearing protocols, then just trust and follow your intuition and let your spiritual support system take the lead. In this sense, you will not interfere with any energetic transformations if they aren't needed. An energy-clearing treatment removes only nonbeneficial energies and will not remove any beneficial ones. Energy-clearing treatments performed with unconditional love are glorious blessings of light for anyone who may experience them, including the person who is lovingly petitioning the energy-clearing treatment. I call them energetic prescriptions of light for the mind, body, and soul.

Distance Energy–Clearing Protocol for Children

Step 1: Energetic Protection and Connection Prayer (Cocreation)

"I ask for divine light protection within and around myself and [state full name of child] as I begin an energy-clearing treatment. I ask for divine light support to assist me in every aspect of [state full name of child]'s energy-clearing treatment today, in harmony with my greatest and highest good, [state full name of child]'s greatest and highest good, and the greatest and highest good of all concerned. Thank you. Amen. It is done!"

That's you linked in, switched on, and ready to go!

Step 2: Energy Test to Check If You Can Begin

With the pendulum in hand, ask aloud if it is appropriate to proceed with an energy-clearing treatment for [state full name, age, and address of child]. The use of their full name, age, and address will help you zone right into their specific frequency and spiritual coordinates. Example: "Is it appropriate to proceed with an energy-clearing treatment for Gemma Davies, five, Kissimmee, Florida?" If you want to look at a photograph of the child as you go through the energy-clearing protocol, then this is perfectly fine.

Step 1: Clear Irrational Fear Energy

With your pendulum in hand, state the following energy-clearing command: "Clear any and all irrational fear energy that's adversely affecting [state name of child] in any way, shape, or form." Your pendulum will begin to move in a counterclockwise direction as it removes any nonbeneficial energies. Once your pendulum has finished moving, then you are ready for the next step.

Step 2: Clear Absorbed Parental–Stress Energies

With your pendulum in hand, state the following energy-clearing command: "Clear [state name of child] of the adverse energetic effects of their mother's and father's stress energies on their entire system." Your pendulum will begin to move in a counterclockwise direction as it removes any nonbeneficial energies. Once your pendulum has finished moving, then you are ready for the next step.

Step 3: Clear Any Childhood Illness Energies
(Including Pain and Inflammation Energies)

With your pendulum in hand, state the following energy-clearing command: "Clear [state name of child] of the adverse energetic effects of any childhood illness energies and of any pain and inflammation energies on their entire system in the highest and best way." Your pendulum will begin to move in a counterclockwise direction as it removes any nonbeneficial energies. Once your pendulum has finished moving, then you are ready for the next step.

Step 4: Clear for Any Learning Difficulties

With your pendulum in hand, state the following energy-clearing command: "Clear [state name of child] of the adverse energetic effects of any learning difficulties (or problems at school) on their entire system in the highest and best way." Your pendulum will begin to move in a counterclockwise direction as it removes any nonbeneficial energies. Once your pendulum has finished moving, then you are ready for the next step.

Step 5: Empower their Confidence

With your pendulum in hand, state the following energy-clearing command: "Empower [state name of child]'s confidence to the highest appropriate level for his/her greatest and highest good." This time, your pendulum will begin to move in a clockwise direction as it works to empower their confidence energies. Once your pendulum has finished moving, then you are ready for the next step.

Step 6: Clear the Environment and Surrounding Area on Their Entire System

With your pendulum in hand, state the following energy-clearing command: "Clear [state name of child] of the adverse energetic effects of their home environment, school environment, and the surrounding area on them." Your pendulum will begin to move in a counterclockwise direction as it removes any nonbeneficial energies. Once your pendulum has finished moving, then you are ready for the next step.

Final Step: Clear and Bless Their Aura

With your pendulum in hand, state the following energy-clearing command: "Clear [state name of child]'s auric field of all forms of nonbeneficial energies, nonbeneficial frequencies, interference, and harm." The pendulum will begin to move in a counterclockwise direction as it clears the nonbeneficial energies. Then state the following blessing: "Bless [state name of child]'s aura with a shield of divine light protection for his/her greatest and highest good." This time the pendulum will begin to move in a clockwise direction. Once your pendulum has finished moving, then you are ready for the closing prayer.

Closing and Grounding Prayer

The following prayer is an example of what you can use. "Thank you to my divine light team (or to my universal support system) for helping me with [state name of child]'s energy-clearing treatment today. Please clear and ground [state name of child]'s energy in the highest and best way; they are now detached. Please clear and ground my energy in the highest and best way. I now detach. Thank you. Amen. It is done!"

Well done—you've just completed an amazing energy-clearing treatment for a child!

Distance Treatments for Pets

Pets also absorb energies from their owner and from the environment. An energy-clearing treatment can help a pet restore their vital energetic balance, overcome health complaints, and feel less anxious. If the pet requires to see a vet for a specific concern, then an energy-clearing treatment can help clear the trauma and shock on the pet from any surgery or treatment. It can also help clear the nonbeneficial side effects of any medication. Pets as well as children are also sensitive to spirit energies, with children being more open to the spirit realm due to their recent incarnation, and with pets detecting an array of energies invisible and inaudible to human consciousness. I have observed remarkable results of pets healing after experiencing an energy-clearing treatment. Willow the dog was diagnosed with meningitis and was in a critical condition. I did one distance energy-clearing/healing treatment for him, and within a period of twenty-four hours he was completely well. His lovely owner stated that "I have a truly remarkable connection with the angelic realm, and because of this I am able to work miracles." She has enormous gratitude and respect for the energy-clearing/ healing treatment I did for Willow, and is overjoyed for Willow's return to health and well-being. Now here's the thing: you also have a remarkable connection with the angelic realm, and you too can help your own sick pet or others, in the following energy-clearing protocol.

Distance Energy–Clearing Protocol for Pets

Step 1: Energetic Protection and Connection Prayer (Cocreation)

"I ask for divine light protection within and around myself and [state name of pet and animal; example: Toby the cat] as I begin an energy-clearing treatment. I ask for divine light support to assist me in every aspect of [state name of pet and animal]'s energy-clearing treatment today, in harmony with my greatest and highest good and [state name of pet and animal]'s greatest and highest good. Thank you. Amen. It is done!"

That's you linked in, switched on, and ready to go!

Step 2: Energy Test to Check If You Can Begin

With the pendulum in hand, ask aloud if it is appropriate to proceed with an energy-clearing treatment for [state name of pet, type of animal, and address]. The use of their name, species, and address will help you zone right into their specific frequency and spiritual coordinates. Example: "Is it appropriate to proceed with an energy-clearing treatment for Toby the cat, Flat Rock, North Carolina?" If you want to look at a photograph of the pet as you go through the energy-clearing protocol, then this is perfectly fine.

Step 3: Measure the Overall Energy of the Pet

Use the energy measurement chart with your pendulum and ask to be shown the overall energy of your pet. Take a note of the measurement.

Step 1: Clear Irrational Fear Energy

With your pendulum in hand, state the following energy-clearing command: "Clear any and all irrational fear energy that's adversely affecting [state name of pet and type of animal] in any way, shape, or form." Your pendulum will begin to move in a counterclockwise direction as it removes any nonbeneficial energies. Once your pendulum has finished moving, then you are ready for the next step.

Step 2: Clear Absorbed Owner Stress Energies

With your pendulum in hand, state the following energy-clearing command: "Clear [state name of pet and type of animal] of the adverse energetic effects of their owner's stress energies upon their entire system." Your pendulum will begin to move in a counterclockwise direction as it removes any nonbeneficial energies. Once your pendulum has finished moving, then you are ready for the next step.

Step 3: Clear Any Animal Illness Energies
(Including Pain and Inflammation Energies)

With your pendulum in hand, state the following energy-clearing command: "Clear [state name of pet and type of animal] of the adverse energetic effects of any animal illness energies and of any pain and inflammation energies upon their entire system in the highest and best way." Your pendulum will begin to move in a counterclockwise direction as it removes any nonbeneficial energies. Once your pendulum has finished moving, then you are ready for the next step.

Step 4: Clear for Any Trauma Energies

With your pendulum in hand, state the following energy-clearing command: "Clear [state name of pet and type of animal] of the adverse energetic effects of any trauma energies and shock upon their entire system in the highest and best way." Your pendulum will begin to move in a counterclockwise direction as it removes any nonbeneficial energies. Once your pendulum has finished moving, then you are ready for the next step.

Step 5: Clear the Environment and Surrounding Area on Their Entire System

With your pendulum in hand, state the following energy-clearing command: "Clear [state name of pet and type of animal] of the adverse energetic effects of their home environment and the surrounding area upon them." Your pendulum will begin to move in a counterclockwise direction as it removes any nonbeneficial energies. Once your pendulum has finished moving, then you are ready for the next step.

Step 6: Raise the Level of Love Energy

With your pendulum in hand, state the following energy-clearing command: "Raise the level of love energy within every cell of [state name of pet and type of animal] to the highest appropriate level for his/her greatest and highest good." This time, your pendulum will begin to move in a clockwise direction as it works to elevate the love energies. Once your pendulum has finished moving, then you are ready for the next step.

Step 7: Clear and Bless Their Aura

With your pendulum in hand, state the following energy-clearing command: "Clear [state name of pet and type of animal]'s auric field of all forms of nonbeneficial energies, nonbeneficial frequencies, interference, and harm." The pendulum will begin to move in a counterclockwise direction as it clears the nonbeneficial energies. Then state the following blessing: "Bless [state name of pet and type of animal]'s aura with a shield of divine light protection for his/her greatest and highest good." This time the pendulum will begin to move in a clockwise direction. Once the pendulum has finished moving, then you are ready for the next step.

Final Step: Remeasure the Overall Energy of the Pet

Take a note of the measurement to check on any improvements in the overall energy of the pet.

Closing and Grounding Prayer

The following prayer is an example of what you can use. "Thank you to my divine light team (or to my universal support system) for helping me with [state name of pet and type of animal]'s energy-clearing treatment today. Please clear and ground [state name of pet and type of animal]'s energy in the highest and best way; they are now detached. Please clear and ground my energy in the highest and best way. I now detach. Thank you. Amen. It is done!"

Well done—you've just completed an amazing energy-clearing treatment for a pet!

Other Kinds of Energy Clearings

There are many kinds of energy-clearing treatments that you can do for smaller environments and circumstances. As always, say a prayer before and after whatever you've decided to energetically clear. The prayer beforehand is for protection and connection with universal support. The closing and grounding prayer afterward is for grounding the energy, detaching from the energy-clearing treatment, and expressing gratitude for the universal support. The following seven mini energy-clearing treatments cover different environments and circumstances that can also be adapted to suit different situations. Example: the energy clearing of appointments can be adapted and applied to the energy clearing of an upcoming interview. All of these mini energy-clearing treatments can be done from the comfort of your own home prior to any travel arrangements or appointments.

CLEAR THE ENERGY OF YOUR CAR (THREE STEPS)

Step 1: Clear the Car's Environment

With your pendulum in hand, state the following energy-clearing command: "Clear my car from all forms of nonbeneficial energies, emotional congestion, and negative thought forms." Your pendulum will start moving in a counterclockwise direction as it clears the nonbeneficial energy. Once it stops moving, then you are ready for the next step. This energy-clearing step can help clear the accumulated stress energies created from any prior arguments within the car, as well as helping clear any trauma energies from any previous traffic accidents or incidents. It also clears the energetic history of the car if it was preowned before you.

Step 2: Raise the Level of Love Energy within the Car

With your pendulum in hand, state the following energy-healing command. "Raise the level of love energy within my car to the highest appropriate level for the greatest good of all concerned." This time your pendulum will begin to move in a clockwise direction as it amplifies the love energy within the atmosphere of the car. This energy-clearing step helps keep the overall energy of your car in a higher elevated vibration, which is super supportive to your personal energies. This step is equivalent to receiving a divine light blessing.

Step 3: Bless the Energy of the Car

With your pendulum in hand, state the following energy-healing command: "Bless my car with a shield of divine light protection to keep myself and others safe from all kinds of negative energies and harm." This time the pendulum will begin to move in a clockwise direction. Once the pendulum has finished moving, then you have finished this mini energy-clearing treatment and you can go ahead and say the closing prayer. This empowering step can help protect the car from any harmful intentions, as well as helping protect those who travel in the car from any possible accidents and incidents.

CLEAR THE ENERGY OF YOUR HOTEL ROOM (TWO STEPS)

Step 1: Clear the Hotel Room's Environment

With your pendulum in hand, state the following energy-clearing command: "Clear my hotel room from all forms of nonbeneficial energies, emotional congestion, and negative thought forms." Your pendulum will start moving in a counterclockwise direction as it clears the nonbeneficial energy. Once it stops moving, then you are ready for the next step. This energy-clearing step can help clear congested energies resonating within the space from the collective history of all who've stayed there before you. Clearing the hotel room's environment in this way can certainly help you sleep more peacefully when spending time in an unfamiliar environment.

Step 2: Raise the Level of Love Energy within the Hotel Room

With your pendulum in hand, state the following energy-healing command. "Raise the level of love energy within my hotel room to the highest appropriate level for the greatest good of all concerned." This time your pendulum will begin to move in a clockwise direction as it amplifies the love energy within the atmosphere of the hotel room. Once the pendulum has finished moving, then you have finished this mini energy-clearing treatment and you can go ahead and say the closing prayer. This energy-clearing step will help keep the overall energy of the hotel room in a higher elevated vibration, which is super supportive to your personal energies and to all others who stay there after you.

CLEAR THE ENERGY OF YOUR FLIGHT (TWO STEPS)

Step 1: Clear the Energy of Your Flight, Destination, and Seat

With your pendulum in hand, state the following energy-clearing command: "Clear the energy of my flight to [state destination] and my seat [state seat number if you know it] from all forms of nonbeneficial energies, interference, and harm." Your pendulum will start moving in a counterclockwise direction as it clears the nonbeneficial energy. Once it stops moving, then you are ready for the next step. This wonderful energy-clearing step can help clear the way for a less stressful journey when traveling, as well as helping clear any fear energy created from other people on the flight, which can cause energetic interference. Clearing the energy of your seat is also beneficial, since you are cocreating a balanced and harmonious space to spend time in during the flight.

Step 2: Raise the Level of Love Energy within the Plane

With your pendulum in hand, state the following energy-healing command. "Raise the level of love energy within the plane to the highest appropriate level for the greatest good of all concerned." This time your pendulum will begin to move in a clockwise direction as it amplifies the love energy within the atmosphere of the plane. Once the pendulum has finished moving, then you have finished this mini energy-clearing treatment and you can go ahead and say the closing prayer. This energy-clearing step will help keep the overall energy of the plane in a higher elevated vibration, which is super supportive to your personal energies and to all others who share the flight with you. You can also do this energy-healing command for your own seat!

CLEAR THE ENERGY OF YOUR MARRIAGE/RELATIONSHIP (TWO STEPS)

Step 1: Clear the Energy of Your Heart/Soul Connection

With your pendulum in hand, state the following energy-clearing command: "Clear the energy of my marriage/relationship and my heart/soul connection to [state full name] of all forms of nonbeneficial energies, interference, and harm." Your pendulum will start moving in a counterclockwise direction as it clears the nonbeneficial energy. Once it stops moving, then you are ready for the next step. This energy-clearing step can help clear any stress energies created both from you and your partner that can interfere with the harmony of your marriage/relationship, plus it can also clear the adverse energetic effects of other people's interference on your relationship.

Step 2: Raise the Level of Love Energy within Your Relationship

With your pendulum in hand, state the following energy-healing command. "Raise the level of love energy within my marriage/relationship to [state full name] to the highest appropriate level for our greatest and highest good." This time your pendulum will begin to move in a clockwise direction as it amplifies the love energy within your marriage/relationship. Once the pendulum has finished moving, then you have finished this mini energy-clearing treatment and you can go ahead and say the closing prayer. This harmonious energy-clearing step will help support your marriage/relationship energy. It can even act as a preventive measure against unnecessary third-party interference when your marriage/relationship is empowered by love.

CLEAR THE ENERGY OF YOUR DENTIST / DOCTOR / HOSPITAL APPOINTMENT (TWO STEPS)

Step 1: Clear the Energy of Your Appointment

With your pendulum in hand, state the following energy-clearing command: "Clear the energy of my appointment with [state whom it's with] from all forms of nonbeneficial energies, interference, and harm." Your pendulum will start moving in a counterclockwise direction as it clears the nonbeneficial energy. Once it stops moving, then you are ready for the next step. This energy-clearing step can help clear any stress energies and interference with your appointment, so that it is more likely to run smoothly without any hitch. Clearing the energy of the appointment in this way can certainly invite your spiritual support system to work through the doctor, dentist, or other in order to best serve you.

Step 2: Raise the Level of Love Energy within the Appointment

With your pendulum in hand, state the following energy-healing command. "Raise the level of love energy within all people associated with my appointment to the highest appropriate level for my greatest and highest outcome and for the greatest and highest good of all concerned." This time your pendulum will begin to move in a clockwise direction as it amplifies the love energy within all people associated with your appointment. Once the pendulum has finished moving, then you have finished this mini energy-clearing treatment and you can go ahead and say the closing prayer. This powerful energy-clearing step will help support your appointment energy and any procedures or tests you are having done. It can even act as a preventive measure against unnecessary treatment when you've invited your spiritual support system to take the lead for your greatest outcome.

CLEAR THE ENERGY OF A COURT CASE (TWO STEPS)

With your pendulum in hand, state the following energy-clearing command: "Clear the energy of my court case with [state all parties involved] from all forms of nonbeneficial energies, interference, and harm." Your pendulum will start moving in a counterclockwise direction as it clears the nonbeneficial energy. Once it stops moving, then you are ready for the next step. This energy-clearing step can help clear any accumulated stress energies, arguments, and interference with your court case, so that it is more likely to run smoothly without any hitch. Clearing the energy of your court case in this way can certainly invite your spiritual support system to work through the legal system in order to best help you. Any spiritual intervention when it comes to justice is always given from the higher elevated perspective of taking into account what's best for the greatest good of all concerned. Sometimes lessons are to be learned all around, and if or when karma is involved, then this also needs to play out without spiritual intervention. In this sense, there is only spiritual support for the best outcome at this time. The next step is even more beneficial when it comes to justice, since it has the power to clear some karmic energies that interplay with all parties tied in any battle.

Step 2: Raise the Level of Love Energy within the Court Case

With your pendulum in hand, state the following energy-healing command. "Raise the level of love energy within all people associated with my court case [including all lawyers] to the highest appropriate level for my greatest and highest outcome and for the greatest and highest good of all concerned." This time your pendulum will begin to move in a clockwise direction as it amplifies the love energy within all people associated with your court case. Once the pendulum has finished moving, then you have finished this mini energy-clearing treatment and you can go ahead and say the closing prayer. This powerful energy-clearing step when done with sincerity (since you may be super annoyed with the other party involved) is one that can be your most beneficial action for a probable positive outcome. Love energy is beyond earthly measure and is unlimited in its levels and supply. When love energy is amplified for the good and best possible outcome for all parties, then you are inviting in divine cosmic healing for complete resolution without any further karmic ties. Sometimes this step is all that is required for this resolution, yet other times it will work more subtly when certain experiences need to happen for higher reasons that our conscious awareness is fully unable to understand at the present time. All becomes clearer as we move through our life and we come to understand that the universe was and is always supporting us in ways that harmonize beautifully with our soul plan, life purpose, and spiritual growth.

CLEAR THE ENERGY OF YOUR FINANCIAL FLOW (TWO STEPS)

Step 1: Clear Financial–Resistance Energy

With your pendulum in hand, state the following energy-clearing command: "Clear any and all resistance energy concerning my finances that block me from going to the next level of abundance." Your pendulum will start moving in a counterclockwise direction as it clears the resistance energy. Once it stops moving, then you are ready for the next step. This creative energy-clearing step can help clear the resistance energy, which can be due to an accumulation of fear energy, debt energy, and interference energy, and will help your consciousness overcome limitations and be more open to receive universal abundance. This abundance energy can manifest as opportunities and experiences for you to go to the next level of prosperity consciousness.

Step 2: Harmonize Your Consciousness with Prosperity Consciousness

With your pendulum in hand, state the following energy-healing command. "I harmonize my consciousness with prosperity consciousness in the highest and best way for my greatest and highest good." This time your pendulum will begin to move in a clockwise direction as it begins to harmonize your vibration and consciousness with prosperity consciousness. Once the pendulum has finished moving, then you have finished this mini energy-clearing treatment and you can go ahead and say the closing prayer. This creative energy-clearing step is one that you can do regularly to help you become more open to attracting and creating greater levels of abundance and financial prosperity in your life. Universal abundance means an abundance of unlimited opportunities and experiences that can lead to you living a life of fulfillment. The intent and goal of this step does not focus on a person having immense wealth and power. It does, however, focus on a person having greater soul freedom within their life experience. You really are an unlimited being of divine consciousness!

CONCLUSION:
WINGS OR WEEDS!

You must not let your life run in the ordinary way; do something that nobody else has done, something that will dazzle the world. Show that God's creative principle works in you.

—Paramahansa Yogananda

I knew that I was dreaming, yet at the same time I also knew that I was being taught some impressive new energy technique within the spirit realm. I watched with fascination as the teacher demonstrated how she could connect with the energy of one environment and then move what looked like to be a portal or vortex of energy to some other location. In this particular demonstration the portal of energy was moved from what I could tell was the face of a big clock tower, traveling over a small lake of water to reach the side of a large building, where it merged with the energy of the building's wall. I didn't recognize where I was, yet the architecture of the place seemed familiar and looked to be Greek. There were other students present who were also observing the demonstration, and we all seemed to be enthralled with what we were learning. I remember saying, "So, I just need to focus with my mind and tell the energy what I want it to do?" The teacher replied, "It's all about your mind power and your vibration. Do you want wings or weeds?" "Wings or weeds," I said. "What do you mean?" She replied, "Do you want wings of light or do you want energy weeds? Wings of light are the created outcome of your mind power generated by your elevated vibration. These wings of light carry the energy waves of your mental intent to the intended destination. Energy weeds, on the other hand, are the attempts you make when you learn to do this technique before you reach the point where you succeed. They lack the creative power it takes to propel the energy waves from its seed of light to its intended area. These seeds of light remain grounded and become energy weeds. I woke up repeating the words "wings or weeds." I asked my husband, "Do you want wings or weeds?" He gave me an odd look and said, "I'd rather have a coffee." Over the years he has become so used to me having unusual and psychic dreams. I have no idea what else took place in that lesson in the Light, or whether I was purposely meant to remember that small part of the dream to include in this book. Yet, what I do know is that there is so much more for us to experience beyond this life than we can ever imagine for us that will enable us to deepen our creative skills, knowledge, and wisdom in our eternal dance with Creation. The unconditional love bonds we share with all others we will always carry with us until we unite once more within the realms of Light.

It was my passion, purpose, and pleasure to write this book to help you with your energy-clearing needs. We are unlimited Spirit beings of love and light energy, and each time we get to clear our layers of resistance to our authentic spiritual nature and the identity of who we truly are, then we will shine our soul's Light ever brighter. It is our Light that enables us to amplify our creative power to attain ever-higher levels of spiritual freedom within this world.

You now have the ability through the knowledge, guidance, steps, and protocols given within this book to take great energetic care of your home environment, your work environment, your business, your relationships, and your personal energies. My goal in sharing my healing expertise with you is to empower you to be able to do this energy-clearing work for yourself and for others. To gently push you forward with confidence in your own creative skills so that you can tap into the wonder of your unlimited spiritual potential. To let you know that you always have benevolent universal support that includes the celestial angels, guides, and universal intelligence.

The creative force of the universe is always guiding you in the highest and best direction for your unique soul journey and life path. It's not a coincidence that you've read this book, since your soul was ready to discover more of its unlimited potential and creative power. My desire for you now is to take your energetic wings of light and to fly high as you enter into the next phase of your life experience. May you always have a Clear Spirit!

—JOANNE BROCAS

ACKNOWLEDGMENTS

I would like to thank my editor Peggy Kellar, along with James Young and the staff at REDFeather Mind, Body, Spirit for their expertise and professionalism throughout the creation of *Clear Spirit*.

ENDNOTES

1 Charles Jennings, director of neurotechnology at the MIT McGovern Institute for Brain Research.
2 James Hutton Institute.
3 Findhorn, Scotland. Peter and Eileen Caddy, along with Dorothy Maclean, unintentionally founded the Findhorn community in 1962.
4 The first notable study in recent history was conducted by Gustav Freiherr von Pohl.
5 Gustav Freiherr von Pohl's book *Earth Currents—Causative Factor of Cancer and Other Diseases*, was published in Munich in 1932.
6 Larry Dossey's bestselling book, *Healing Words: The Power of Prayer and the Practice of Medicine* (New York: HarperOne, 1995).
7 Olgar Worrall: "I Refuse to Hurt Them."
8 Dossey, *Healing Words*.
9 The Hollywood film *The Men Who Stare at Goats*.
10 Hanna Kroeger, *The Pendulum Book*.
11 Christopher Bird, bestselling author of *The Divining Hand*.
12 David Hawkins developed a well-known map of consciousness (Hawkins 1995, Power vs. Force).
13 Eugene Maurey's book *Exorcism*.
14 Bill Finch in his excellent thesis on spirit possession, "The Pendulum and Possession."
15 The Bovis scale is named after a French researcher, Anton Bovis.
16 *New York Times* bestselling author Dr. and Master Zhi Gang Sha.
17 Film adaptation of the Broadway musical *Chicago* (2002), as the murderous nightclub singer Velma Kelly.

ABOUT THE AUTHOR

Joanne Brocas is an expert healer, intuitive, and number one best-selling author with over thirty years experience in her field. Joanne is passionate about teaching others all about the life-changing power of energy clearing, spiritual healing, and intuitive development. You can find more about Joanne's Clear Spirit workshops, classes, and courses by visiting her website www.joannebrocas.com